Dick Kinzel
Roller Coaster King
of Cedar Point Amusement Park

*A Legends & Legacy Biography
by Tim O'Brien*

CASA FLAMINGO
Literary Arts

"I found out very early in my career that the harder I worked and the more hours I worked, the luckier I got."
- Richard L. Kinzel

Copyright © 2015 by Tim O'Brien. Printed and bound in Nashville, TN, U.S.A. All rights reserved. No part of this book may be reproduced or transmitted in any form or by any means, electronic or mechanical, without prior written permission from the publisher at **Books@casaflamingo.com**

Reviewers may, and are encouraged, to quote brief passages in a review to be printed in a magazine, newspaper or on the web, without written permission. Tear sheets and/or links to mentions are appreciated.

Published by Casa Flamingo Literary Arts, Nashville, TN
www.casaflamingo.com

Paperback first printing, October, 2015
ISBN: 978-0-9743324-6-8
Library of Congress Control Number: 2015950594

Cover, Page and Text Design: Jennifer Wright
Production Director: Tim O'Brien
Distribution: Ingram Global Publisher Service

For additional copies of *Dick Kinzel – Roller Coaster King of Cedar Point Amusement Park,* ask your local bookstore to order or purchase online at www.casaflamingo.com or www.amazon.com Distributed by Ingram and available throughout the US, Canada, Australia, United Kingdom, European Union, and Russia. For quantity discounts contact **Legends@casaflamingo.com**

TABLE OF CONTENTS

Foreword – 4

Part One: The Man and His Climb to the Top - 5

Part Two: The King's Creations - 30

Part Three: Rounding out the Package - 58

Part Four: Dick's $2 Billion Spending Spree - 69

Part Five: After the Spending Spree - 97

Selected Bibliography - 116

Acknowledgements - 119

About the Author - 120

Index – 121

FOREWORD

I first met Dick Kinzel on a trip to Cedar Point in 1987. It was his first summer as the company's president and CEO and I couldn't have asked for a better reception than he and his staff provided that day. I spent several hours with him in the park and knew when I left that I had just spent time with a very special person. Our friendship grew over the years as I interviewed him countless times and rubbed elbows with him and his wife Judy at industry events around the world. It's been a pleasure over the past year to have had this opportunity to write a biography not only about a friend, but of an industry legend.

As you will read, his story is one of tenacity, conservatism and risk taking. It's one of big business and one of fun making. Dick has spent his life putting smiles on people's faces and fear in their eyes. During his thirty-nine year career, he built the world's first 200, 300 and 400-foot tall roller coasters. He brought big, edgy and expensive coasters to Cedar Point knowing that the bigger the thrill ride, the bigger the crowds. He made sure Cedar Point remained the Coaster Capital of the World.

During the many hours we sat talking in his lakeside home, just steps from the front entrance of Cedar Point, Dick told me his story. He told me of great times and of his huge successes and he openly shared with me his failures, disappointments and embarrassments. What started out as a biography of one great man evolved into a history of Cedar Point during the nearly four decades under his leadership. Much of that story is being told here for the first time.

Thanks Dick. Now readers – hop on and strap in for a truly fascinating story with all the ups and downs of the world's biggest, fastest and longest roller coaster! Enjoy.

Tim O'Brien
October, 2015

PART ONE:
The Man and His Climb to the Top

Richard "Dick" Kinzel fired the first shot in the Coaster Wars.

That initial volley was in the form of the creation of Magnum XL-200, the world's first roller coaster to top the two hundred foot mark. It premiered at Cedar Point in Sandusky, Ohio on May 6, 1989. The thriller helped set a park attendance record, it brought coaster aficionados in from around the world and it showed other park operators that bigger could be better.

Coaster fans quickly spread the word praising the 205-foot tall, 72 mph Magnum XL-200 using superlatives such as bodacious, stupefying, mind-altering and humongous. The ride established Cedar Point, located on the shores of Lake Erie, as the Roller Coast and as the Roller Coaster Capital of the World. It also established Dick Kinzel as the Roller Coaster King of Cedar Point and later as the monarch of thrill rides at all Cedar Fair parks.

During his thirty-nine year career at Cedar Point and Cedar Fair, Dick brought the biggest, longest, tallest and fastest roller coasters to Ohio. By 1990 the park had more coasters and more rides than any other park on the planet, operating one of the best mixes of traditional and contemporary rides in the world.

The Coaster that started the Coaster Wars of the 1990s – The Magnum XL-200. (Cedar Point Photo)

Cedar Point has never been nor probably ever will be a theme park. It's an amusement park with a lot of rides.

People who visit don't want theming, they want to ride big rides. Dick points out that he saved money by not needing to theme rides to satisfy his guests. And by saving money, bigger and better thrill rides could be purchased.

The rides weren't themed, but each had its own personality achieved through its uniqueness, its visual placement, colorful design and appealingly designed ride stations. A great deal of thinking went into each name chosen for each ride. Dick only tried to theme a ride once, and that was a disaster, literally. More on that later.

"We did coasters and thrill rides right. We knew if we went big and fast and went after screams and thrills, we could pack the park year after year." That's exactly what he and his team did. An Arrow Development Corkscrew in 1976 started Cedar Point on its quest for the best. "The Corkscrew showed us to the path that we followed. If we build it big, they will come."

The 102 year-old Cedar Point was a sleeping giant in 1972 when Dick joined the company. It already had a celebrated history but it needed a man of vision and determination to see beyond a single amusement park on Lake Erie; to imagine and create an entertainment empire that now stretches from the Atlantic to the Pacific and into Canada.

That man turned out to be Richard Lee Kinzel. When he took over as president and CEO in 1986, Cedar Fair was a $100 million company with two parks and a hotel. By the time he retired at the end of the 2011 season, it was a billion dollar company with eleven amusement parks, five hotels, seven waterparks and a marina. His unmatched fiscal leadership grew the company in a conservative, focused way. By the early 1990s, Dick had boosted Cedar Fair's profit margins to 29 percent, more than double (then) industry leader Disney's profitability.

Born in Toledo, Ohio in 1940, Dick began his career at Cedar Point in food services, moved to operations a few years later and became the park's director of operations in 1975. He soon learned the knack of picking out great thrill rides. He became VP and general manager of Valleyfair in Shakopee, Minn. when Cedar Point bought that property in 1978. He went back to Cedar Point as top dog in 1986 and with deep pockets resumed his search for the biggest, tallest and fastest.

By the time Dick retired, hundreds of millions of rides had safely been ridden on the thirty-seven coasters he had been responsible for creating at all eleven Cedar Fair amusement parks.

Disney Didn't Take Him

After high school, Dick attended La Crosse (Wisconsin) State Teachers College for one year, before dropping out and returning to Toledo where he married his high school sweetheart, Judy Guy (he was twenty, she was eighteen). He quickly secured a position with the Canteen food-service company and worked his way up to commissary manager.

Always a hard worker with a blue-collar work ethic which he learned from his tavern-owner father, Dick jumped into his new job, eager to work. "I always liked to work." He started helping out his dad as a soda pop bottle sorter when he was six or seven, and then after a few years, Dick was "allowed" to mop the floors. The other kids in the neighborhood would be outside playing but Dick says he didn't mind at all being inside washing dishes, peeling potatoes, or doing whatever he was asked to do. "It gave me a true sense of accomplishment."

Dick grew up in a staunch German/Irish Catholic family in a Democratic Irish Catholic neighborhood, where, he notes, the "Republicans were the rich ones." He says he can count to this day, on one hand, the number of times he has missed Sunday Mass over the years. "When I was a bit older, I would work on Saturday nights with dad and mom at the tavern. We would be open until around 2:30 a.m., then we'd clean up the bar, have breakfast, and go to the 6:30 a.m. Mass. We would then go home and go to bed. I loved every minute of it."

In early 1971, when he was pulling in a yearly salary of $12,000 at Canteen, he had two copies of his resume prepared. One, he sent to Walt Disney World, which was getting ready to open in Central Florida, applying for a position in the food service department. At the same time, he learned there was an opening in Cedar Point's food department and he sent the second copy to them.

Disney officials responded saying they "do not have a position for which we are able to consider you." He still has that letter. He didn't think Cedar Point was going to respond at all, but one day when he was outside painting his house in Toledo, he heard from them. It was a call that was almost never made. His resume ended up in the seasonal personnel office and was thrown into a "rejected" pile of applications. Bev Ontko, secretary for Bill Near, the director of food services, went to the office looking to hopefully find an assistant for her boss and found Dick's resume in the cast-offs. She liked what she saw and took the resume to Near and the call was made. He was offered $14,000 a year and he accepted immediately.

Walt Disney World Co.

A Subsidiary of Walt Disney Productions

P O BOX 40 • LAKE BUENA VISTA, FLORIDA 32830
TELEPHONE (305) 828-3333

March 22, 1972

Richard Kinzel
1539 Craigwood
Toledo, Ohio

Dear Richard:

Thank you for your recent inquiry regarding employment at Walt Disney World.

We have carefully reviewed your background in light of our present staffing requirements and feel at this time that we do not have a position for which we are able to consider you. I regret we are unable to be more encouraging. However, please be assured that we will contact you should the opportunity develop.

We appreciate your interest and thank you for sharing our enthusiasm for Walt Disney World.

Very truly yours,

WALT DISNEY WORLD CO.

Thomas J. Eastman
Employment Manager

TJE/lab

Cedar Point, Inc., Sandusky, Ohio 44870 (419) 626-0830

"Everyday is Funday at Cedar Point"

May 9, 1972

Mr. Richard L. Kinzel
1539 Craigwood Street
Toledo, Ohio 43612

Dear Richard:

In regards to our recent conversations concerning employment with Cedar Point, Inc. As per our conversation, this is not a seasonal position.

You would be hired as a Food Service Supervisor and after a trial period of three months you will be evaluated for the position of Assistant Manager of Food Services.

Starting salary would be Fourteen Thousand Dollars per annum.

Reasonable relocation expense from Toledo, Ohio to Sandusky, Ohio would be covered by Cedar Point, Inc.

You would be qualified to participate in our company insurance program after a thirty day employment period. Cedar Point, Inc. absorbs approximately one-half of the insurance expense.

I would appreciate your response to this offer at your earliest convenience.

Yours truly,

CEDAR POINT, INC.

William E. Near, Director
Food Services

cc: T. B. Woodworth

WN/bao

Dick, circa 1972.

It was June 6, 1972 and he was thirty-one years old when he began his amusement park career as assistant manager of food services. He stayed in company housing at the park, visiting Judy and his four children who remained in Toledo, when he could. Interstate United had the food contract for all of Cedar Point at the time and Dick was hired to help phase out that company and bring food services back under the Cedar Point flag. He was put in charge of the commissary and initiated buying procedures for the department.

Two years later in 1974, many of the full time employees were recruited by Marriott's new park division to help build and manage three new parks. Major reshuffling was required at Cedar Point due to that unforeseen mass exodus. Bill Near took over as VP of both the Cedar Point food services and operations

CEDAR POINT, INC., SANDUSKY, OHIO 44870
(419) 626-0830

RICHARD KINZEL
Asst. Manager, Food Services

departments, Dick was promoted to director of food service and by the end of 1974 the contract with Interstate United had been terminated. But Dick was restive and ready to move on to another challenge.

After working in food service his entire adult life, Dick felt it was time for something different and he applied for a position within the operations department. "With so many people leaving for Marriott, and I thank them for that by the way, there were several job openings in operations."

He thinks his brief answer to one big question during his interview for the job secured it for him. He was asked to describe what the operations department did. "I told them that operations is responsible for the guest from the time they come into the park until they leave." He had heard Truman Woodworth, the former park president, use that description in an earlier meeting. It worked for Dick and he was hired into operations and spent the first three months of 1975 studying ride policy and asking a multitude of questions.

Woodworth, a twenty-two year veteran of the Disney parks, joined Cedar Point in 1970 as VP and was the heir apparent to take over for the park's aging management team of George Roose and Emile Legros. When Roose retired, Woodworth was appointed president, but was one of those who left to join Marriott in 1974. Legros took over but died in early 1975 and long term board member and big investor in the company, Bob Munger was poised to take over as president and general manager.

That spring, both Munger, who owned an insurance company and knew very little about running a park, and Dick who knew nothing about operations were on a learning curve. "I was ready by the time the park opened in May," Dick said. "But I still had a lot to learn and I surrounded myself with people who knew a lot more than I did." He kidded with a reporter several years later that when he walked into the park on his first day in operations, he "didn't know a coaster from a carousel."

Dick's knowledge was limited, but his eagerness was immense. He recalls an event that took place during his first season in operations. "I was equipped with a radio and when I heard that a ride went down, I hurried to that ride to help out. But it didn't take me long to realize that once I got there I couldn't do anything until someone who knew what they were doing showed up."

Having listened to Munger's consistent messaging that everyone needed to consistently be conscientious about expenses, Dick thought he had hit the payload during his first year in operations. He was in charge of buying coal for the steam locomotives at the park. Oil, gas and even coal had skyrocketed in cost so Dick searched for an alternative source from which to buy the coal. While the coal the park was buying was priced at approximately $90 a ton, Dick found a source selling it for only $17 a ton. He bought two train cars worth of the less expensive coal, not realizing there were different grades of coal from which to choose.

Park guests started complaining about soot from the locomotives getting in their eyes and on their clothes, complaints that had never before been heard at the park. He soon discovered that the cheap coal was totally the wrong type and it was making a mess of everything, so he had to make another purchase, this time buying the right coal. It never occurred to him there was a difference. "I thought coal was coal." By mixing the cheap stuff in with the proper coal a little at a time, Dick's coal pile lasted for nearly ten years before being burned up.

Dick Learns Big is Better

Lee Jewett, the park's VP of planning and design, heard of a new type of coaster that had been installed at Opryland Theme Park in Nashville, Tenn. He and Dick visited the park, rode the Wabash Cannonball and liked what they saw, felt and heard. The coaster was a Corkscrew, built by California-based Arrow Development. It had premiered in

1975 at two parks - Knott's Berry Farm in Buena Park, Calif., and at Opryland.

The Cedar Point Corkscrew was Dick's first coaster purchase. (Tim O'Brien Photo)

Arrow president and chief ride designer Ron Toomer was contacted and a deal was struck up for a Corkscrew to open at Cedar Point the following season. It was the first coaster on which Dick and Jewett worked together and their instructions to Toomer were simple. "Just add another element to what you have at Opryland and make it bigger and better and we'll take it." A loop was added and it opened the following season, on May 15, 1976 and it was a huge success.

The $1.75 million coaster was the first ride to turn people upside down in the park and within a week of it opening, meetings were called to figure out how to queue the guests so they wouldn't block the midway. The success caught management by surprise. By the time the 102-day season was over, attendance had topped the three million mark for the first time ever, essentially putting Cedar Point on the map.

The ride nearly didn't make it to the starting line. The night before the opening, Toomer and his team were running and testing the ride when two trains collided in the station. No one was riding so no one got hurt. Luckily, it was a three train operation and the maintenance guys worked all night cannibalizing parts from the two crashed trains to build one good train. Two trains were in operation by the time the park opened and only the Arrow and Cedar Point teams knew of the mishap. If that had happened in today's safety conscience park environment, the ride would never have been allowed to open on schedule.

The path of the Corkscrew also caused another, not oft-spoken about problem. The ride went out and over part of Jungle Larry's Safari's elephant compound. Within a day the elephants began to have diarrhea. Dick said he doesn't recall how that issue was solved.

Most parks at the time had ride entrances located on the busy midway and the ride itself went away from where the crowds were, back into the trees where the real estate was cheap. That kind of layout was effective land use but it would virtually hide the elements. On the Cedar Point Corkscrew, "Dick came up with the elements he wanted and I placed the ride," Jewett said. "I wanted the elements to be visual, to be spectator friendly." What they ended up with was a ride in which people who didn't ride could still get involved, and share and feel the experience vicariously. Unlike the Wabash Cannonball at Opryland whose helix was located at the back of the ride out in the woods where no one but the riders could see it, Jewett placed the helix directly over the midway where guests would walk under it. Dick liked the placement and encouraged Jewett to use that same approach on every ride he helped create at every Cedar Fair park.

Based on the record attendance and the media attention the Corkscrew brought to the park, Dick immediately started shopping for another record breaking coaster, and found an idea he loved - a twin racing coaster. He sold the idea to Munger and Ron Toomer was called.

Opening in late June 1978, Arrow's twin tracked racing Gemini premiered as the tallest and fastest coaster of any kind ever built. With a 125-foot lift and a drop of 118-feet, the 3,935 foot long (per side) ride had a huge capacity, running six, thirty passenger trains. Another attendance record was set that year. "We followed the formula. Give them something big and exciting and they will come." By then, the park had five coasters in operation and people started appreciating there were a lot thrills at Cedar Point. (Coaster designer/builder Arrow Dynamics had many names through the years in which it worked with Cedar Point and Cedar Fair, including Arrow Development and Arrow-Huss. To avoid confusion, we will simply call the company Arrow throughout the rest of this treatise.)

The twin-tracked, racing coaster, Gemini.

The $3.4 million Gemini was huge in comparison with other coasters at the park. The dark, tall wooden structure cast an ominous shadow over the midway. At the time, Toomer had never built a steel coaster that tall and had never built a wooden coaster. After overcoming several engineering challenges, he decided upon the unique wood structure/steel track concept. It is still only one of a handful of coasters worldwide constructed in this manner. The wooden structure gives it the look of a massive traditional wooden coaster and the tubular steel track gives the ride the smoothness and versatility of a steel coaster.

Cedar Point Not for Sale

During 1977 and 1978, several park companies, including Taft Broadcasting, owner of Kings Island near Cincinnati, and Marriott reached out to buy Cedar Point but deals never materialized. However, with millions in cash on the balance sheet and very little debt, the park was a plum takeover target. Lou Wasserman, then head of MCA Recreation Enterprises, parent company of the Universal Studios Tour in Hollywood, notified Munger that he was about to make a serious play for Cedar Point in early 1979.

In defense, Munger used most of the cash on the balance sheet to purchase Valleyfair in Shakopee, Minn. for $15 million along with some assumption of debt, which meant that most of the cash on the balance sheet was no longer there. Wasserman, not wanting two parks with little cash on the books, stepped aside.

Munger wasn't gung-ho about buying

Dick and the Rockettes at Valleyfair in December 2005.

Valleyfair at first. Dick recalls him asking why they should expand when "we're already making more than General Motors." Dick laughs when he recalls that conversation. "Yes, he was right, we had a 40 percent margin and the company had a lot of money, which nearly led to our doom." Quick thinking by Munger saved Cedar Point and in the process, the company made its first acquisition, which is still in the family today.

The Valleyfair purchase was official in September 1978 and Munger faced a unique problem. He couldn't get any of his Cedar Point vice presidents to move to Minnesota to run the park. Munger phoned Dick over Labor Day weekend and offered the position of VP and general manager of Valleyfair and Dick immediately accepted it. By Wednesday of that week he was in Minnesota meeting his new team. "We all learned by trial and error and took a lot of ideas to reality. It was done by taking a really good team and letting them do what they wanted. That's what made us successful."

In his first interview at Valleyfair after joining the park, Dick pointed out the property had great potential for growth. "We will combine what has been learned by the people here and what we have learned at Cedar Point. What will result will be the best of two worlds." That was his outward bravado speaking, but he was both concerned and a bit afraid of what he was about to face.

For the first time in his career, Dick realized what he didn't know could affect his performance. He had only one year of college and only six years of park experience and now he was the general manager of an amusement park. Going in, he was totally aware of his biggest weaknesses - finance and marketing.

During the first couple months at Valleyfair he would sit down with the park's chief financial officer and would ask a lot of questions, hoping to be able to understand the park's finances better. After an early June meeting with the CFO on capital and general financial questions, Munger summoned Dick to Cleveland and told him to bring Judy along. The Valleyfair CFO, who Dick had spent a good amount of time with had written Munger a letter criticizing Dick, expressing to Munger that Dick was not capable of running a park.

It was a scary time for the thirty-eight year old. "I knew nothing about the letter so I was puzzled why Bob wanted me to sit down with him face to face. And why he wanted me to bring Judy." They arrived at Munger's home and Dick was shown into his home office. Munger then suggested that Judy and his wife go shopping for several hours. It was cut and dry. "He handed me the letter and I read it. He asked me if I knew what I had to do. I said I had to go back and fire the CFO and he smiled and shook his head and that was it. He said it was time for

Dick and Valleyfair VP/GM Walt Wittmer. (Tim O'Brien Photo)

his nap and he left me alone in his office for a couple hours. We all had dinner that night together and nothing more was said about the letter." They flew home and at the end of the next day Dick fired the CFO, a task he didn't want to do but one that was inevitable. The CFO's only comment was, "Why did you wait until five o'clock?"

Judy laughs as she recalls that trip. "As we were headed to Cleveland the only reason I could figure out why I had to come along was to bring home the body." It all worked out, but the whole situation had Dick in a big worry. "I had a great job I loved that I didn't want to lose. I was shaking like a leaf."

Buoyed by Munger's faith in him, Dick jumped back into his Valleyfair adventure and built a strong team. "Throughout my career, I wanted people around me with whom I could trust and they in turn needed to be capable of trusting me and willing to fall on a sword for me if necessary." At Valleyfair, Cedar Point, and eventually at all Cedar Fair parks, internal communication and trust were keys to Dick's success. His teams were encouraged to openly talk with each other and once a week they would gather for a meeting and hear about what all the other departments were doing. "It was our strength."

Venture capitalists built Valleyfair and had opened it in 1976. Two years later when Dick joined the team, the park was grossing approximately $8 million annually. By the time he left in 1986, it was NETTING more than $8 million a year. Attendance during Dick's reign grew from less than eight hundred thousand to more than a million. The same formula that worked for him at Cedar Point was soon put into action at Valleyfair and an Arrow Corkscrew was installed in 1980. It was the park's second coaster, joining the High Roller wooden coaster that opened with the park four years earlier. Similar to Cedar Point's Corkscrew with a loop as an added element, Valleyfair's Corkscrew was positioned over a lagoon and its corkscrew elements twisted over a walkway. The people loved it and in a way, that coaster also put Valleyfair on the map.

He looks back at his days in Minnesota as an eight year training period that prepared him to take over the entire company. "I was involved in everything at Valleyfair and I learned a great deal about all the departments involved in making an amusement park work. When I had the opportunity to go back to Sandusky as president and CEO, I was ready."

He Learned by Walking

Dick is known throughout the industry as the leader who would rather be in the park than behind his desk. His desire to spend time out walking and talking with both guests and employees was a part of his strength and popularity as a leader and a main ingredient to his success. He loved walking in the parks and seeing people enjoying themselves. "After all, we're in the fun business.

Dick spent a lot of time talking with his staff during daily walks in the parks. (Cedar Point Photo)

It also allowed me to get a good feel for what was going on. Once we had several properties, I could walk into one of them and know immediately if something was wrong. I knew the parks, I knew the business and I knew when something was not right simply by observing the park's cleanliness, the attitude of the employees, and just the overall feel of the place."

One can thank Dale Carnegie for making Dick so personable. He was a shy kid and was never much of a communicator as a young adult. At some point in his early career at Canteen, he was advised he should take a Dale Carnegie course that would help him come out of his shell and help him communicate better. He said the course gave him the confidence that he needed. His thirst for knowledge never ended. During his Canteen days as well as his early years at Valleyfair and Cedar Point, Dick took non-matriculating night classes at several universities in subjects ranging from finances to computers to salesmanship.

The fact that he was a college drop-out was always a non-issue with his bosses as well as the media. When the media would ask about college, "I would always tell them the truth and I would add that the board didn't know it and I would prefer they wouldn't find out. They never wrote about it." He joked that one reporter could have scooped everyone else by writing about his lack of a formal education. He said he could just see the headline that was never written. "Non-College Kid Running Cedar Fair."

Dick "graduated" from the People Management School at Walt Disney World in 1988.
(Walt Disney Company Photo)

A big part of his continuing education consisted of visiting other parks during the winter months, most notably the Walt Disney World parks in Florida. "That was mecca for me. They seemed to do everything right and I would walk the parks and take it all in. I knew we could never compete with them as far as capital is concerned, but I knew we could match them in quality and service." In 1988, he attended the "Disney Approach to People Management" seminar to acquire an even better understanding of the Disney way.

Dick Joins Ownership

Munger, who was then chairman, president, and CEO, was getting concerned about new takeover bids and in 1983 Cedar Point's attorneys told him that the company, now with two parks, was positioned nicely for an LBO (leveraged buyout). In March of that year, Munger told Dick that an LBO was in the works and that it would take the company private and in the process, repel all takeover quests.

Eleven Cedar Point executives were invited to be a part of the buyout. The new company included both parks and was to become Cedar Fair (CEDAR Point and ValleyFAIR). Each of the eleven participants could buy up to ten units, with each unit costing $10,000. At the time it was permissible to borrow money to invest in an LBO and Dick took advantage of that option and purchased the entire ten units. Key Bank financed the management debt. Lazard, a financial advisory firm in New York City helped finance and organize the LBO and put several of their own people on the Cedar Fair board.

For the next three years, Dick remained Valleyfair VP and general manager, as well as part of the ownership group. Going back to Cedar Point was the farthest thing from his mind when Dick received a phone call from Cedar Fair board member David Veit in mid-December, 1986. "I was curled up on the couch watching a Saturday afternoon football game when I got the call asking if I would be interested in going back to Sandusky and if I would be interested in having a high position within Cedar Fair." Not sure of what was being offered, Dick told Veit that after running his own park for this long that he "couldn't come back as a second fiddle." The voice at the other end assured Dick he wasn't going to be second fiddle to anyone. "No, this is for the number one position for Cedar Fair," said Veit.

"When do you want me there," was Dick's swift response.

He and the ten others who had formed the LBO, all now owners of the company, gathered in Cleveland and Dick was introduced as the president and CEO of Cedar Fair, a position he held until he retired in early 2012. He also held the title of chairman of the board from 2003 to 2010.

By early 1987, the LBO had accomplished what it had been set up to do – protect the parks from a takeover. Lazard, the financier behind the LBO, now wanted the return on their investment, and it was decided to take the company public, choosing a master limited partnership that would be traded on the New York Stock Exchange under the symbol FUN. The eleven who were involved in the 1983 LBO became general partners, and shares of limited partnerships were put on the market. Proceeds from the public offering went to the original stakeholders in the LBO, Lazard and several individual investors. Less than a year later Munger lost his battle with cancer and died at age fifty-nine.

Dick, circa 1987.

Cedar Fair, L.P. was now a public company and subject to all SEC rules and regulations. Lazard also sponsored Cedar Fair going public and invested by buying shares in the company. This allowed them to invest at the start and get out any time they wanted simply by selling their units. A master limited partnership trades shares known as units on the New York Stock Exchange. The initial price of one unit, or share, was $10 when the company started trading in 1987.

Being a public company has its good and bad elements, Dick said. The company now had a responsibility to both a board of directors and individual investors (unit holders). That added a level of required transparency to an operation and the added obligation to meet certain SEC regulations.

Everyone is required to know your business when you are a public company. It is requisite to make public all capital plans and in doing so, the company loses a little of the competitive edge they had when they were private. In general, Dick says, "You have to disclose so much information that everyone knows your basic business. There can be no real surprises."

Dick Comes into his Own

Media stories about Dick and Cedar Fair nearly always pointed out three things: the reality that big steel attracts big numbers, that through his focused management Cedar Fair created some of the largest margins in the industry, and that the top management team within the company had been together for a long time adding both stability and expertise to the business. In a *Forbes* story in fall 1991, reporter Lisa Gubernick begins her story describing Dick. "Kinzel is upright, plain-spoken, has a firm handshake, (and) wears a drip-dry short-sleeved shirt." She continues and explains the great financial shape the parks are in, noting that "much of this success is the work of Richard Kinzel" due to his "inspired management."

Dick stops to look over the landscaping near Gemini during one of his walks in the park.
(*Sandusky Register* Photo)

Jewett, the park's VP of planning and design from 1963-2002, said Dick's return to Cedar Point as top man brought a brand new and refreshing work ethic to the park. "For years, we had absentee management, whether they lived in Toledo or Cleveland or somewhere in between, our president or general managers didn't spend much time here and were never hands-on. With Dick, not only was he more involved, he lived right next to the park, within steps of the front gate. Plus he worked very long hours not only in his office, but he walked the parks consistently and knew the product probably better than any of our managers of the past."

Bob Masterson was president of Ripley Entertainment and served with Dick on the board of the International Assoc. of Amusement Parks & Attractions (IAAPA) and visited him at Cedar Point on several occasions. He says Dick always seemed to have a special relationship with the people in his company. "When you walked the park with Dick you could feel the respect they had for him, and in return, the respect and affection he had for each of them. He was, and still is in retirement, one of our industry's most respected leaders."

Dick's work ethic combined with his long-tenured team was also noted by John Raitt, a partner at Harris Associates investment firm in a 1996 article in *Kiplinger's Personal Finance Magazine*. "They eat, breathe and live the amusement park business and with the exception of maybe Disney, they're really the class of the industry."

The name tag simply read "Dick," but his dress shirt and tie usually gave him away as management. The dress code for all supervisors, managers and executives was simple - they were required to always wear a tie while in the park. How else could the guests tell the chiefs from the Indians? "It was important guests could spot us and approach us if they needed to ask or tell us something." He very seldom, if ever carried a radio and there was no clipboard. However, he would occasionally take notes to share with his managers at the proper time.

In its write-up about Dick winning the Register Award, a kudo that honors individuals for service and commitment to the Sandusky, Ohio community, Evan Goodenow of the *Sandusky Register* wrote: "He's a hands-on workaholic, but he knows when to delegate authority. He is conservative and frugal by nature, but his biggest successes were huge risks. He is outgoing and personable but will play tough when he has to. Like many successful leaders Dick Kinzel has his share of contradictions."

He loved the park environment, but the original reason he would spend so much time out walking is that he wanted to be there if anything happened. It wasn't micromanagement, he insists. He wasn't out there looking for problems, he just wanted to be easily available if there were any.

The background to that philosophy made sense to him. "Even after I became CEO I was scared of losing my job. I didn't want anything to get out of control. I believed that if I saw something small, I could keep it from getting large. In my early days, I figured if I didn't see something happen and I wasn't there and it got out of hand, and (Bob) Munger found out about it, he would come down hard on me and I didn't have enough confidence in myself at that point to handle that kind of confrontation."

And Dick wasn't the only one out walking around. "I didn't like people having offices, I wanted to see them out in the park, reacting to people's needs and wants. You would hear things and you could react immediately if you had to. Not being responsive to the needs of our guests is a sure way to kill our business. People are not going to return to a park that doesn't meet their expectations."

Michigan TV reporter Jim Geyer praised Dick in a blog posting in June 2008 following an interview in which he took a short walk with him through the park. "I like people who make things happen, make things work, enjoy their work and maybe, most importantly aren't full of themselves. Are all CEO's like this? Unfortunately not, but I'm glad the CEO of a company with a stock symbol FUN is interested in making sure that people who are paying money to visit Cedar Fair's parks are having fun."

Tim Baldwin, a journalist with *Amusement Today*, said he has seen lots of general managers out in their parks, but his walks with Dick at Cedar Point felt different. "You could really see his love for the park environment in his demeanor."

Dick often did what insurance companies tell their insured not to do – communicate with anyone hurt in an accident at the park. "If I was around and someone would get hurt or have to go to the hospital, I would often go check on them because I was honestly concerned about them. I found it amazing that if people know you are worried and show some interest in them they'll think twice before blaming you or suing you."

Major changes have taken place through the years and no matter how much bigger the rides and attractions are today, Dick feels the basics of the park industry have not changed. "Take the lipstick off any park and underneath, it's still a carnival. Disney changed the appearance of parks in the 1950s with Disneyland, but we are all still operating dressed up carnivals." Which is not all bad, he adds, "Because a basic carnival, set up to put smiles on people's faces is still at the root of all entertainment today."

Back to Ohio

While his two oldest sons, Brett and Bart remained at college in Minnesota, Dick, Judy along with their daughter Stacy and son Derrek moved back to Ohio in late 1986. They lived in Cedar Point housing in Sandusky while their new home was being built, directly adjacent to the parking lot of the park. He bought two Lake Erie lakefront building lots from Cedar Fair and Lee Jewett designed their home. It took a year for phase one of the house to be completed. Dick considers it the first phase because he has built onto the structure five times since. Hating debt as he does, he would build on whenever he got a nice bonus. Jewett made sure everything always blended together. Now empty nesters, Judy and Dick still live in that house with a sandy beach and great views across Lake Erie.

Standing in the Kinzel's yard, the view directly forward is of their beach and the expansive lake. At night, looking off to the northwest, the lights of the busy park can be seen through the trees and the screams from the Gatekeeper coaster, located at the front gates of the park, can be heard faintly in the background. "You'll never get Judy to move from here, but there will be no more additions added. The days of the bonus are over."

PART TWO:
The King's Creations

While Dick was building up the ride arsenal at Valleyfair, Munger added Avalanche Run, an Intamin bobsled coaster on May 11, 1985 to Cedar Point and had on order an Arrow suspended coaster to be named Iron Dragon, which premiered June 11, 1987. Before he left Valleyfair, Dick had Thunder Canyon, a white water rapids family ride under construction and that ride is credited for taking attendance over the one million mark in 1987, for the first time in that park's history.

By 1987 Dick, now Cedar Point's top man, knew how to leverage the formula that had already proven itself to him several times. Go for the superlatives of fastest and tallest and you'll have a winner. There are three major reasons why it's nice to be able to claim big records when adding a thrill ride: additional thrills to the ride lineup, increased attendance, and marketing value. It had now been eleven years since the Gemini had opened at Cedar Point and Dick felt the park was due for another record-breaking coaster.

To create a world-class ride, Dick says, one doesn't have to be a genius. "You just have to talk with the right people, come up with a plan and have enough gumption to go to the board and ask for the millions of dollars to build it."

Fresh off the public offering, the park had an abundance of cash and Dick knew exactly how to spend it. Bring on the superlatives! It's that time again.

Coaster fans' love affair with Dick began with the appearance of Magnum XL-200 in 1989. They loved him because he listened to them and was able to give them what they wanted. Journalist Paul Ruben, the North American Editor of British-based *Park World* magazine recalls Dick telling him that he credits members of the American Coaster Enthusiasts (ACE) with the idea to build Magnum. "He saw video clips of Bandit, a 167-foot tall coaster that had just opened in Japan. An ACE member was interviewed and he raved about the ride. He said it had no corkscrews or helixes in it, and it didn't go upside-down. It was just a fast, smooth ride—one of the best coasters he had ever ridden."

Dick subsequently asked some North American ACE members if the public would accept a coaster that went high and fast and had a lot of thrills, a lot of speed bumps, a lot of camelbacks, but didn't offer any 360-degree loops or other inversions. They all agreed that a coaster like that would go over quite well in the U.S. That was all the research Dick needed.

While Arrow's Ron Toomer was in the park building the Iron Dragon, Dick questioned him about the height of the tallest coaster in the world. Toomer noted that it was the 170-foot tall multi-element Shockwave that he was then building for Six Flags Great America near Chicago. Dick asked him if he could top that and Toomer agreed with no hesitation. Dick also talked with TOGO, the Japanese-based company that had built the Bandit, but because of the weakness of the dollar at the time, the price was higher than Dick wanted to pay.

The $7 million price tag Toomer presented needed to be approved by the board and when Dick proposed building a 187-foot tall coaster to set the record, a board member asked why stop at 187, why not go over 200? How much more will that cost? Dick went back to Toomer for the answer. To his surprise he found it would only cost an additional $100,000 to add that extra height. The board immediately told him to "go for it."

Dick wanted to call the new coaster Magnum, but Jewett suggested that a more descriptive name be used. "Why not add XL for extra-long and a 200 to connote that it tops 200 feet," asked Jewett. That was it, the tallest, fastest roller coaster ever built was to be called the Magnum XL-200. It also created a new category for defining a coaster –

hypercoaster, meaning that it is over 200-feet tall with no loops or inversions. The ride was a hit then and has splendidly stood the test of time. Nearly thirty years after being built, Magnum is still an alluring and popular ride in the big steel skyline of the park. One journalist in 2014 called the twenty-five year old Magnum a "perfectly conceived thriller."

Who designed the Magnum? Dick said he left it up to the imagination of Toomer and his team. It was an easy request. Cedar Point's instructions to the ride builder were simple: build a fast ride with a lot of G-forces with no three-sixties or helixes. Toomer took it from there. In his biography written by this author, Toomer said of all the eighty-plus coasters he built and designed, the Magnum XL-200 "stands out as one of the best rides I ever created."

It was early Saturday morning, April 29, 1989, a week before the Magnum XL-200 was to open and the trains still had not made an entire circuit. Dick walked up to the ride platform just as Toomer was getting ready to release the

The Magnum XL-200 at dusk. (Cedar Point Photo)

train that was to be the first one to run a complete out and back. The group watched it run a successful route and as it came back into the station, Toomer looked at Dick and said, "Okay, hop on for the first ride." No sand bags, no second run. It was just Dick and a couple of the maintenance guys with Jack Falfas in the station at the controls.

The ride was fast and as the train went into the last turn before heading into the station the trim breaks didn't work. The ride held to the track, giving everyone a safe but scary ride. Dick was exuberant but later admitted that he had never been as scared on a coaster as he was going into that curve. The ride opened as scheduled the following weekend with less than a week's testing. "That would certainly not be allowed now," Dick notes. Today, it takes weeks of testing and hundreds of circuits completed before anything other than sandbags can ride.

Avid coaster rider Alan Shick said that while the Magnum XL-200 certainly helped Cedar Point, it also had a huge effect on virtually every major amusement park in the world. "I like to say that Mr. Kinzel fired the first shot in the coaster wars because once other park companies saw what a big coaster could do for the profits and reputation of a park, many others followed. They all went for the records and we coaster riders ended up with some great rides as everyone out there tried to outdo everyone else."

America's RollerCoast

The Magnum XL-200
(Cedar Point Photo)

The 205-foot tall, 72 mph Magnum XL-200 was a triumph, and it was another record year for the park. Within the 130-day operating season, the $7.5 million (final cost) coaster added $10 million to the park's bottom line, literally paying for itself in one season.

The huge success of Magnum was an emotional touchstone for Dick, according to marketing VP John Hildebrandt, and had his imprint all over it. Once Magnum opened, Hildebrandt noted, "We all were smart enough to know we had something. Big steel made a big difference and with Magnum we started branding ourselves as a big time roller coaster park." Dick admits it was one of his riskier moves and recognized in an interview just before his retirement that if Magnum "had bombed," his career would have been very different.

One of Dick's favorite stories centers on the board of directors and the Magnum. The board was in the park for a meeting in June 1989, the opening year of the famed coaster. He came up with a fun idea and had a little prank set up ahead of time. He invited the board to ride, shamed them into it, and had Jack Falfas at the controls with instructions to stop the train for ten seconds or so when it reached the very top. The board was seated in the first five rows and board member David Veit and Dick were in the front seats. When the train stopped, Dick turned and told the board that it was time to discuss management's bonus program. "I could only see fear in their eyes, and I remember Veit saying, in his British accent 'Kinzel, you bastard' as the train went over the top of the hill. No one ever forgot it."

Thanks to the Magnum XL-200, park attendance topped the three million mark for the fifth time during 1989 with 3.2 million coming through the gates.

All capital additions and improvements at all the parks in which Dick had oversight during his career were paid out of cash flow. "We never went into debt during those years and once we set a budget for the season, we were careful never to go over it."

Dick, along with Lee Jewett, left, and Don Miears, gives a thumbs up to the idea of staying on budget and on time. (Tim O'Brien Photo)

They occasionally had to make adjustments along the way, but "we met weekly on the budget during the season and were able to adapt to the unseen expenses as they came along." He said none of the myriad projects during his career got to the point where he had to go back to the board for more money. "He was a very smart and thrifty manager," Hildebrandt said. "His key responsibility in a project was to control costs and he was very good at it."

Dick stayed on budget partially because he always required his lead on the project, typically Lee Jewett, to communicate honestly on how much capital was needed. "I always told Lee to give me a Cadillac and let me break it down to a Ford if I needed to cut costs, but don't give me a Ford and keep telling me what else is needed to make it a Cadillac." In other words, don't come in cheap to get the project approved and then keep coming back for more money to be able to complete the project successfully.

As a self-described "expense freak," Dick hated all waste and the spending of money when not absolutely necessary. That's one reason he used very few consultants during his career, preferring to solve issues in-house. He was known to have a temper and several people, including Jewett, pointed out that the best way to see Dick lose it was to mismanage a project. "I took a lot of pride in having the best margins in the industry and if I saw waste anywhere in the park, I would easily lose my temper," Dick said. "My anger never lasted very long. I said what I had to say and got it out of my system and then apologized if necessary."

Although he knew big and tall brought big numbers, capital expenditures and the marketing for 1990 were directed more to families than thrills. Money was spent on new attractions for Soak City waterpark, a couple children's rides and a brand new family-oriented hotel, Sandcastle Suites. Also, 1990 was the first time costumed characters made their way onto the Cedar Point midway. Father, Mother, Sister and Brother Bear – the Berenstain Bear family – were there to meet and greet the small kids near Kiddy Kingdom. Families at Valleyfair were treated with a new ride, the $1.2 million Minnesota Valley Railroad. The combined attendance was down by 4 percent at the two parks for 1990, but revenues were up slightly across the board.

An independent research project showed that people thought of Cedar Point as more of a thrill ride park for younger people than a family friendly park that had something for everyone. The Bears were a success with families that first year and based on their popularity, The Berenstain Bear Country children's area was added in 1992 and remained popular until 1999 when it was replaced by Snoopy and the Peanuts characters. The Bears remained alive and well in similar areas in Dorney Park and at Valleyfair but have all now been replaced by Peanuts-themed children's areas.

Disaster by Dick

Dick was at Valleyfair when Munger and his team decided to build the bobsled run and he makes it clear that he had nothing to do with it. But he does take full credit for adding insult to injury in what he calls his biggest mistake ever.

"When I first rode Avalanche Run, I thought it was the dumbest ride I had ever ridden. It was terrible and it's a good example of putting a horse into a committee and having it come out as a camel." When the ride was proposed, park operations required it to have a certain capacity; the safety department required it to have certain alterations to satisfy safety concerns; and marketing wanted it to be flashy enough to help sell the park in 1985. "They took a mediocre ride and made it a dog," Dick said.

In 1990, Dick's idea was to enclose the aforementioned ride, add theming and rename the "dog" coaster Disaster Transport and promote it as a family experience. A $4 million investment covered the ride and added themed elements to the inside. "I put a big box around a junk ride and we ended up with a junk ride inside a big box." It was his first and his last go at major theming.

The way he dealt with the press during the media preview day for Disaster Transport is an indication of why the media always seemed to like (and trust) him. "This thing was a disaster and they knew it. If I had told them that it was the latest in technology and that within five years it was going to revolutionize the coaster industry, they would have known I was blowing smoke." He preferred to be honest with them. Dick maintained the highest respect for the media because he knew they were only doing their jobs, mostly on a strict deadline, so he made himself available. He would talk with them and if they asked questions he couldn't answer for proprietary sake, he would simply tell them he could not answer that question at that time. He would never lead them away from the truth and would never tell them a lie. Did he use "no comment" a lot? "Oh heavens no, that's so Richard Nixon."

Looking for a Beast

As he was still smarting from the Disaster Transport debacle, Dick contacted Charles Dinn who had built the wildly popular Beast wooden coaster at Kings Island near Cincinnati in 1979. Dick asked Dinn and his designer Curtis Summers to build the world's tallest wooden coaster at Cedar Point. "No problem," Dinn assured Dick. "We will outdo the Beast."

The world's tallest woodie was ordered and that's what they got; the $7.5 million Mean Streak topped out at 161-feet. It did okay, and still does, but it is far from a great coaster. "Building the Mean Streak was not a mistake. We needed a wooden coaster and we were hoping for a Beast. But it was never on the same planet as the Beast. Nothing has ever come close to the Beast."

Dick and Judy following the first ride on the Mean Streak.
(Cedar Point Photo)

Dick likes to joke that he could have started a lumberyard with the amount of wood in the Mean Streak. Covering 5.5 acres of land, the ride consists of nearly 1.7 million board feet of lumber. That's more than enough to place it in a single line from Sandusky to Chicago.

Park officials knew immediately they didn't have a great coaster. It was high maintenance and several sections had to be modified almost immediately in part due to its rough ride. Water hoses had to be turned onto the structure to prevent expansion and contraction in the heat and to keep the wood from splitting. Unlike the other major coasters added at Cedar Point, Mean Streak had little, if any impact on attendance. In fact the gate count was down 1 percent in 1991, but revenues were up slightly.

Through the years, Dick learned to love the excitement of coaster riding and would often take several rides a day as he walked the park. "But when I would ride the Mean Streak, I had to stop for the day after just one or two rides. It was that rough."

B&M Comes to the Point

By the early 1990s, the Swiss company, Bolliger & Mabillard (B&M) had started making a name for itself by designing and building big, unique coasters. Walter Bolliger had talked with Dick at the amusement park trade shows but had never offered anything that excited him. In 1992, the first of the Batman-themed rides opened at Six Flags Great America, near Chicago, and a team from Cedar Point, including Dick, visited the park to experience it. It was the world debut of the first B&M inverted coaster, which meant people sat under the track with their feet dangling. Coaster buffs like to say "nothing but air beneath your chair."

Don Miears, then executive VP at Cedar Point was part of the team who travelled to Chicago to see the ride. "It was very intense. We exited the ride and we all had to lean against the fence while our equilibrium returned. It was a great ride, but there were too many elements too close together." Miears remembers advising Dick that "if we stretched it out a bit and made it longer, even with the same elements, it is a ride we should have."

Bolliger was contacted, discussions ensued and Cedar Point ended up with an inverted coaster that was a taller and longer version of the Batman ride with the addition of a new element – the cobra roll. The $11.5 million Raptor opened May 7, 1994. During the official announcement, Dick predicted to the media that the ride, the park's eleventh coaster, would set the pace for the next century of roller coasters and would long be remembered for changing the look of Cedar Point. With a BIG presence near the front gate, Raptor helped set a record of 3.6 million visitors for the season, a record that still stands in 2015.

No other ride in Cedar Point history up to that point, not even the Magnum in 1989, created such excitement in the marketplace. "Our customer surveys that year proved we had done something spectacular. Our scores were 4.85 on a 5.00 scale," said Dick, noting at the time that the park's eleven coasters "are the greatest collection of coasters in the world." While he loved what Raptor did for the park, he pointed out in late 1994 that his all-time favorite ride, the Magnum "is still the king of the hill."

The Biggest and Best

Coasters had proven to be people magnets and by now Cedar Point was in the middle of the coaster wars with other parks around the world. Dick set out to be the biggest and the best and by now, that's where he was, on top with more coasters and more thrill rides than any park on the planet. The park proudly marketed that position promoting that it had "more than one hundred rides and attractions." It was a position he wanted and there was never any doubt in his mind that his journey to bigger and better coasters would continue. He made it clear that he would do whatever was needed to stay both the biggest and the best. He said the size of the park and it's three million plus attendance could financially justify such purchases because each would have the proper return on investment.

With record crowds in 1994, thanks to the Raptor, Dick noticed there was a need to diversify offerings. The coaster lines were getting very long and realizing that not everyone liked coasters, management diversified ride options in 1995, the park's 125th anniversary, and put in additional kiddie, family and thrill rides, some of them just to eat up capacity and help eliminate the long lines on the other rides.

However a funny thing happened. No matter how many rides were added, the lines for the top coasters never ebbed. People came for the coasters; the lines remained the same.

He liked the quality of B&M products as well as the results they provided, so Dick sat down with Bolliger and came up with another steel coaster that would keep the park at the top of the coaster wars. Mantis opened on May 11, 1996 at a cost of $12 million. It opened as a record breaking stand-up coaster. Once again, Dick was not too specific in his request. He didn't tell B&M  engineers what he wanted except to say it needed to be different, bigger and taller and faster than any other standup coaster in the world. B&M delivered once again with unique elements and inversions for a standup that had never been done before. It would be Cedar Point's twelfth coaster and it would be renamed over the years three times, twice within the first month.

The most recent name change was in 2015 when it was reworked into a floorless coaster and renamed Rougarou, a werewolf-like creature of French folklore. Originally, in 1996, the ride was to be named Banshee, a creature of Irish folklore. T-shirts and other souvenirs, press kits, and a colorful logo were not only designed, but created and printed. A problem with the name surfaced less than a week after the official announcement when Dick learned of the real meaning of Banshee. "As soon as I found out what it meant, I stopped everything and told them that no matter what it cost, we were to never use that name while I was still around." Somehow the marketing team forgot to disclose the full definition of Banshee when they presented it to Dick.

Hildebrandt remembers the moment when Dick found out the true meaning. "He wasn't the kind of manager who interfered with what we were doing nor did he second guess us but this is one of a very few times he stepped in and pulled the plug. There was no negotiating. There was to be no Banshee," he said.

A Banshee is: "A female spirit whose wail was said to foretell death." Dick claims that marketing had failed to tell him about the "foretelling death" part – not a concept one wants associated with an amusement ride. As can be imagined, the name change brought about as much publicity as the announcement of the ride itself the week before. *Sandusky Register* columnist Michael Throne might have had more fun with it than any member of the Fourth Estate. "Isn't a roller coaster's name supposed to be imposing and suggest some type of fear?" One of his readers suggested a new name: "How about The Big Steel Scary Thing?" The reporter's neighbor suggested "The Teenager" and Throne admitted that his neighbor's suggestion was "REALLY scary."

Dick presents Congressman Paul Gillmor with a very collectible Banshee T-shirt.

Banshee was renamed Mantis. James Spencer of the Lorain *Morning Journal* noted that "Cedar Point has renamed its newest roller coaster Mantis, after the most voracious predator of the insect world." Park publicist Stephen Norton told Spencer that officials had no problem with changing the name from Banshee to naming its ride after a carnivorous insect whose female population has the habit of biting off the heads of its mates. Norton pointed out that the female mantis consumes its prey while standing up. "We felt that was very fitting for a stand-up roller coaster," Norton was quoted as saying.

Dick said the entire Banshee naming debacle garnered the park more press over naming a ride than any other coaster or thrill ride he had ever been associated with. An *Associated Press* story with the headline "Banshee too Macabre for

Cedar Point," ran in dozens of papers across the country. The *Chronicle Telegraph* of Elyria, Ohio ran "Cedar Point Praying for its New Mantis." The Jackson (Michigan) *Citizen Patriot* proclaimed that "Cedar Point Scared by Banshee."

True to Dick's wishes no ride or attraction was ever named Banshee while he was at Cedar Fair's helm. However, three years after Dick's retirement, Kings Island, a Cedar Fair park, named its new $24 million coaster Banshee and embraced the legend, going as far as creating a Banshee Brew Festival in June 2015, two months after the coaster opened to the public.

Buckeye Homecoming

The 1996 season was the tenth anniversary of Dick's arrival back to Cedar Point in his new role of president and CEO. It had been a busy ten years. During the decade, more than $100 million had been invested at Cedar Point including seven major rides including four world-class coasters; a major water park; a new hotel; and a major renovation and expansion of Hotel Breakers. Those impressive numbers don't include the attractions and coasters he built at the other Cedar Fair parks.

Dick continued to love hypercoasters. The Wild Thing, a mile-long, 207-foot tall, $10 million steel coaster was added to Valleyfair in 1996; Dorney Park set attendance and revenue records in 1997 with the addition of the tallest coaster on the East Coast at the time, the $10 million Steel Force; and Worlds of Fun received the $10 million Mamba in 1998. The three rides were very similar in ride, speed and length and cost to the father of the hypercoaster, Magnum XL-200.

It wasn't a difficult decision for Dick to add these Morgan Mfg. behemoths. "We knew our guests loved them, we knew they were highly marketable and we knew 200 foot was the magical number." Even though the rides were similar in height and length, each was different due to the terrain being different in each park. Each ride offered a different experience, thanks to that contour.

In his letter to the board and to investors in the 1998 Cedar Fair annual report, Dick pointed out that "major thrill rides drive our business, but in the long run a park needs a balanced blend of rides and attractions to be successful. Something for everyone may sound like a cliché, but it does reflect that our parks serve a family market of great diversity." He then pointed out that "Cedar Fair's $48 million capital improvement program for 1999 reflects a balanced investment in new rides and attractions based on the needs of each park."

That investment for Cedar Point was the park's thirteenth coaster, a Vekoma junior steel coaster named Woodstock Express was added to the new Peanuts-themed Camp Snoopy. People were starting to wonder if Dick had forgotten about big steel. It had been three years since Cedar Point introduced a record-breaking coaster. They didn't know it, but he had something very big in the works to celebrate the new millennium.

Most Anticipated Coaster of the Century

The $25 million Millennium Force opened on May 13, 2000 as the tallest and fastest continuous circuit coaster in the world. Towering at 310-feet tall, the ride reaches 92 mph over its 6,595 feet of track. It was the first 300-foot tall coaster in the world and lured by the park's superlatives – tallest, fastest and the first-ever - people came from around the world to experience it.

With its opening, Cedar Point was able to lay claim to ten world records, including most steel coasters at a park, the most total rides in a park, and the most coaster track in a park - 44,013 feet. That's more than eight miles of coaster track. When announced, Millennium Force was quite likely the first coaster ever that had people wondering, "Is this thing going to be TOO intense for guests? Will it be too intimidating?" Even some coaster fans were asking, "How big is too big?" In the end, it did not scare guests away, the lines were long and along with another very good season the

> *Some in the amusement industry wonder whether the new coaster will attract more people than it intimidates.*

The Toledo *Blade* posed the big question.

coaster solidified Cedar Point's position as the world's premier roller coaster park. The coaster war was ongoing and Cedar Point had won another huge battle.

How did coaster fans react? Did they like it? Starting the year it was built, the Millennium Force ranked consistently as the number one or number two steel coaster in the world each year as voted by the readers of the popular *Amusement Today*.

It became the fourteenth operating coaster at the park and was the most expensive single-ride investment ever made at Cedar Point. The steel giant got the attention of a worldwide audience. *Park World*'s Paul Ruben attended the opening and noted the following. "No park has done a better job than Cedar Point to fuel the increasing popularity of roller coasters. Millennium Force is the seventh record-setting ride the park has unveiled (since 1989)."

Discussions had been underway with another manufacturer to build the ride, but according to Dick, engineers were not able to solve two major issues – "how to get the cars to the top quickly and how to come up with a more durable material for the wheels." Sandor Kernacs of Intamin, along with the help of the park's VP of maintenance and construction Monty Jasper, was able to solve the issues and Intamin ended up with the contract.

Jasper and his team of 120 headed up construction and had the ride ready in time for the park opening in 2000. "On time and very close to budget," points out Dick.

Millennium Force created a new phenomenon at Cedar Point. "So many guests arrived early to ride it that we had to create a holding area just inside the main gate to avoid a crush at the turnstiles." Following the National Anthem and

The Millennium Force, the first coaster to top the 300-foot mark.
(Cedar Point Photo)

as the gates opened every morning, "hundreds of guests" took off running down the midway to get in line at the new coaster. Dick says "they sprinted like they were in training for the US Olympic team." The staff would stand back and watch what they called the running of the bulls.

In 2002, another new coaster was added to the Cedar Point lineup, but Dick's plans for 2003 were so big and so expensive for the following year, that he had Intamin install a less expensive double-impulse shuttle coaster with an LIM launch system. There was a similar ride, Steel Venom at nearby Geauga Lake, but Dick added his imprint on this one by having its two columns twisted instead of a straight up run-out and a few extra feet added to each column. He describes the ride as a "fill-in" coaster, but was still able to call it "the tallest, fastest, double-twisting impulse roller coaster in the world." Twister opened on May 5, 2002 at a cost of $9 million.

World's First 400-foot Thriller

Top Thrill Dragster, Cedar Point's 2003 entry into the coaster wars, was receiving a great deal of worldwide interest even before it opened. In a tourism story in February, LaRaye Brown of the *Sandusky Register* wrote: "Since the amusement park announced its Top Thrill Dragster ride on January 9, the Sandusky/Erie County Visitors and Convention Bureau has received twice as many requests for information from groups considering coming to the area." Janice Witherow, a park spokesperson at the time would not comment on specifics but was quoted as saying there had been a significant jump in job applications since the ride announcement.

Before the official announcement in January, speculation worked overtime during summer and fall of the previous year about what the next coaster was going to be. On the Internet, coaster fans were having a field day guessing and speculating. Cedar Point marketing played into the speculation by installing a webcam to stream the step-by-step construction of the yet unnamed and undefined ride.

Dick tried a new approach to his ride announcement policy on Top Thrill Dragster. In an interview with this reporter for *Amusement Business* in October 2002, he said. "We're trying something new this year. For now, we're only saying it's a major thrill ride so our marketing people will have something to promote for our season pass sales." Dick was obviously enjoying the mystery when he hosted a gathering of park officials during the fall meeting of the International Assoc. of Amusement Parks & Attractions at the park in September 2002. He was asked about the big yellow supports rising above the trees. "Oh, those? That's the base of the golden arches for the world's largest McDonald's," he kidded.

The descent of the Top Thrill Dragster. (Cedar Point Photo)

While it was good for publicity, Top Thrill turned out as the most troublesome coaster Dick had ever brought to one of his parks. It was the most difficult to get open and keep open because of its revolutionary design. It spent more time not working than operating that first year, disappointing hundreds of fans who drove to the park specifically to ride it. Things got better the second year, and it didn't start running reliably until the third season. The $25 million Intamin thriller is 420-feet tall and launches passengers from 0 to 120 mph in four seconds. It is the first coaster to top the 400-foot tall mark and it was the fourth time Cedar Point set a roller coaster height record.

"We knew right away we had a home run. We had a coaster that beat all others and if you didn't want to ride it, which we found that 50 percent of our guests didn't, we put up a small grandstand for those who preferred to watch." The ride was placed along the midway, allowing non-riding guests an easy opportunity to watch others as they were blasted out of the station.

In an interview with the Cleveland *Plain Dealer*, Dick admitted that building the Top Thrill Dragster was the "dumbest decision" he ever made as CEO. He said because of the price and the technical problems during the first couple years, he would never do it again and predicted that the public would never see anything like it in any of the other Cedar Fair parks. "We break everything out by cost per rider. That's far and away the most expensive ride we have in the park to run." He said Cedar Point had a good reputation for having all the rides running with little downtime and this one didn't live up to the billing. "Keeping the large rides and coasters open, without sacrificing safety was definitely our top priority in all the parks."

Even though it broke down a lot, the ride was a marketing bonanza for the park in 2003. More than one thousand media showed up for the park's official media day and results from the park's satellite press kit alone accounted for twelve million impressions the first weekend. The excitement of the ride helped increase Cedar Point attendance in 2003 by 3 percent, up to 3.3 million visitors and increased occupancy at the park's resort properties by 5 percent.

"We really could not have justified that kind of expenditure at any of our other Cedar Fair parks. Here, the coaster promoted the park and helped us fill our hotel rooms. It created a worldwide interest in our resort and that's a very important and valuable part of the package we have to offer."

Following the installation of Top Thrill Dragster in 2003, Dick worked to fill a need for non-coaster thrills at all the parks. The MaXair, the thrill ride added to Cedar Point in 2005 was created by Huss Park Attractions and is only one of two Giant Frisbees in existence, the other being Delirium, added at Kings Island in 2003. Both were unique to the lineup at both parks when built. The ride swings in a pendulum motion while rotating clockwise. At the peak, riders reach a height of 140-feet above the ground although the structure of the ride stands at only 84-feet tall. The pendulum motion propels riders back and forth at 70 mph.

Another unique ride added at Cedar Point in 2006 allowed marketing to use its superlatives once again on a non-coaster ride. Skyhawk is a Screamin' Swing ride built by S&S Worldwide. The structure is 103-foot tall at its highest point, making it the world's tallest swinging thrill ride at the time. At full swing, the ends of the arms approach 125-feet above the ground at a maximum velocity of 65 mph.

While Dick was running the company, the formula was to build a new major thrill ride every two years at the large parks; the smaller parks every four years. For Dick, "major" usually meant a roller coaster. The back to back additions of the non-coaster rides MaXair and Skyhawk in 2005 and 2006 at Cedar Point was unusual. "We already knew Maverick would be coming in 2007 and we had a great line-up of coasters already, so we figured a couple very tall thrill rides would help add some great diversity, especially for the non-coaster thrill seekers. They were both received very well."

The Maverick Brothers

Maverick by name, Maverick by nature

OK, it's not the tallest, the fastest or the scariest, but Cedar Point's new ride may well be the one that will have coaster enthusiasts excited next year for its uniqueness.

From an editorial in the Sandusky Register praising the new coaster.

"Cedar Point has once again set itself apart from the rest of the amusement park industry – and named its new, one-of-a-kind coaster accordingly. After nearly one year of speculation, the park revealed early this morning that Maverick – a $21 million terrain-hugging coaster that whips passengers dangerously close to the ground – is the mystery ride being built in the northwestern corner of the peninsula." That's how the *Sandusky Register* announced that season's new ride on its front page on Sept. 7, 2006. The Western-themed ride opened on May 26, 2007

Definition of maverick: independent in thought and action.

The innovative terrain coaster didn't set any records for fastest, tallest or scariest, a fact that appeared to be defended in a *Sandusky Register* editorial on Sept. 14, 2006. "True to its name, the themed ride is a step away from the roller coaster path CP (Cedar Point) has dominated for decades. When other parks are building higher, faster, steeper coasters in an effort to catch up to Cedar Point, the maverick minds at CP are looking to appeal to a broader group of fun seekers. To our way of thinking, Cedar Point has again proven they are on the cutting edge of amusement park thrills."

Top speed of the Intamin ride reaches 70 mph, seconds after its second launch by linear synchronous motors (LSM), the first coaster in the park to offer that launch technology.

Top height is 105 feet. Dick said they were looking in a different direction for this coaster and it gave them the diversification that they needed and wanted. It was the park's seventeenth coaster and its sixty-ninth ride.

Dick takes credit for naming the western-themed ride. His favorite TV show during the late 1950s was *Maverick*, starring James Garner. He liked the show so much, he and Judy's first two sons were named Brett and Bart, the Maverick brothers on the TV show. Dick named the trains on the Maverick coaster, Bart, Brett, Samantha and Beau, the four top characters in the show. "Judy put a stop to me naming the kids just in time, because she knew that our daughter Stacy would be Samantha and our third son Derrek would be Beau if she had let me continue."

Rethinking the Woodie

In 2007, the $6.5 million 97-foot tall Renegade, a Great Coasters International product became Valleyfair's second woodie and the first built at a Cedar Fair park since Mean Streak at Cedar Point in 1991. Why would Dick build another wooden coaster in his land of giant steel machines when his last experience with a woodie wasn't the best? "We were told that Great Coasters had solved many of the maintenance issues that plagued wooden coasters and were able to create a comfortable ride for the guests. We went and took a look and liked what we saw. They built us a great ride."

Great Coasters International was called in again to build the $8 million 102-foot tall Prowler at Worlds of Fun in 2009. With Mean Streak, Cedar Point went for the height records and it gave the marketing department an opportunity for bragging rights but at the same time, it gave the maintenance department many, many headaches. "We got what we wanted with Mean Streak, but at 161-feet tall it is just too extreme for a wooden coaster if you want a comfortable ride. That's why we stayed around the 100-foot mark with the subsequent woodies we built."

Officials of the family-owned Morey's Piers were interested in adding their first wooden coaster to their popular pier parks in Wildwood, N.J. Jack Morey and his brother Will, visited Cedar Point to check out the coasters and to ask Dick for his advice. "When we asked for his guidance, he emphatically said he would never build another tall wooden coaster as long as he lived and he went on to explain the problems they had with the Mean Streak. As a result we decided to reduce the height of our then proposed coaster and we switched the frame to galvanized steel instead of wood. We opened the Great White in 1996 and thanks in part to Dick, it remains our number one ride."

Dick is quick to give credit to not only his own in-house team of coaster builders headed up by Monty Jasper, but three others who through their creative coaster building helped him make Cedar Point the Roller Coast of the World. Sandor Kernacs of Intamin, Walter Bolliger of B&M, and Ron Toomer of Arrow all contributed greatly to the records the park established over the years. Toomer went on record several times during the years saying he always looked forward to working with Dick and his team at Cedar Point.

With the billion dollar debt from the Paramount Parks purchase, combined with the economic downturn which started in 2008, Dick said he made the concentrated effort to not invest in major rides until things turned around. The formula of adding major attractions every two or four years was changed to an "as needed" model.

Ironically, the last major ride Dick put into Cedar Point was not a coaster. It was the WindSeeker, a 301-foot tall flying swing ride, by Mondial Rides. After a month of construction delays due to bad weather, the ride opened next to Lake Erie on June 4, 2011. Dick liked it because of its height and its uniqueness and of course the grand look of its structure. The lighting package provides a spectacular sight from anywhere in the park at night, and the view from the top is the best in the park.

The Coaster King

From 1986 through 2011, Dick signed off on thirty-seven major coasters including seven over 200-feet; three over 300-feet; and one over 400-feet. Dick and his team always worked from a rolling five-year plan and the last major coaster on his five year plan when he retired was Fury 325, a 325-feet tall B&M hyper-coaster that opened for the 2015 season at Carowinds in Charlotte, N.C. Also on that five year plan when he left was another 300-footer to be built at the back of Cedar Point, but that coaster was scrapped for the $25 million Gatekeeper B&M winged coaster now at the front gate. "They changed it, which is fine because that's a very good coaster."

Dick and Don Miears at the Mantis.
(Tim O'Brien Photo)

Dick has always been a favorite among park and coaster fans and in return, he has enjoyed his interaction with them over the years. The event now known as Coaster Mania was started by Cedar Point in 1989 to celebrate fan's interest in everything roller coaster at Cedar Point. Held each year in early June, the event typically draws more than 2,000 fans from coaster clubs around the world. With park admission and a small charge for lunch, fans enjoy special ERT (exclusive ride time) when only the registered fans are permitted on the rides, thus providing the opportunity to ride more coasters more times without time-consuming lines.

During lunch, Dick or other park officials would join the group, offer an official welcome, and take the opportunity to meet members of this special group. "These are the people who know parks and coasters and they are the ones who vote each year in the Golden Ticket Awards, so we always wanted to give them the opportunity to experience our rides and our park. Their voting leads to the awards we have won and those awards have provided us with great promotional opportunities. To be a big park and win as many awards over the years as we did, you need to have a lot of positive press and a great openness with your guests."

Tim Baldwin, a knowledgeable coaster fan as well as the Golden Ticket Awards communications coordinator for *Amusement Today* said Dick very seldom missed the awards ceremony, held each fall. "He really enjoyed accepting the awards on behalf of the park and he always gave members of his team the opportunity to accept them on stage as well. He loved to hang around and talk with coaster fans."

Although Dick saw it as a smart business decision, he stayed away from charging park guests, other than for special events such as Coaster Mania, for the privilege of cutting lines and going to the front without waiting. Most parks started this policy years ago but Dick did not feel right about it. "None of the Cedar Fair parks had special queues to allow people to just walk up and get on the ride. People who have waited in line for an hour or more don't like to see others walk by them and get right on, even if they had to pay extra for that right."

While many of the parks today (now including Cedar Point) offer such a "Fast Pass" type privilege for up to $95 per person per day, on top of already steep admission prices, Dick wonders about the long-term effect on park goers. "I do have to admit it is a good revenue generator and is very popular, but the idea of people with money being able to buy that extra privilege bothers me." Not only does the sale of the passes create extra revenue, but it frees guests up to spend more time in shops and eateries, which will help increase revenue as well. It's hard to spend money while standing in a line.

He made the early decision to not follow Six Flags or Disney's path down what many call the privilege ticket. Dick and his team experimented with several free concepts that would allow guests to shorten the amount of time spent in line and the one that worked best, Freeway, was a color-coded hand stamp. The guest would walk up to the ride and get a stamp that would designate when to come back and ride without needing to stand in a line. Once that ride took place, they could go to another ride and do the same.

Dick and NASCAR Star Jeff Gordon on the Millennium Force in 2009. (Cedar Point Photo)

Dick agrees that not charging for that privilege was "leaving gold on the ground." But that didn't mean he felt it was right.

PART THREE:
Rounding Out the Package

Beer gardens, water slides, a bathing beach, a dance pavilion, a twenty room hotel, and the area's first roller coaster were all part of the Cedar Point peninsula prior to 1900. Over the years, the park had always been more than just a place to ride rides and have fun – it was a destination. The park's lakefront setting, the white sandy beaches and the activity of the park itself provided all the elements needed for it to become a popular site to visit.

In 1901 a second hotel was added and four years later in 1905, the grand, six hundred room Hotel Breakers premiered. Under owner George A. Boeckling, the park entered into what is now known as the Golden Age of Cedar Point.

That Golden Age had tarnished by 1947 when Boeckling's company was nearing bankruptcy and officials declared that "the conditions here are hopeless." Local businessman Dan Schneider became manager of the resort and was able to hold the company together and keep it out of bankruptcy. Ten years later, George A. Roose and Emile A. Legros purchased the majority of the Boeckling Company and along with it, the control of the park. The causeway (now the Richard L. Kinzel Causeway) from the mainland to the park was completed in 1957 allowing easier accessibility without relying on public transportation.

Dick's Links to the Past

It is in 1957 that the "modern" Cedar Point era begins under the direction of Roose and Legros. In 1972 when Dick began his career, both park owners were still alive and active. And while he never reported directly to either, he did know them. When Legros died in 1975, Munger replaced him as president and CEO and that year, Munger moved Dick into operations.

"While I appreciated everything that Roose and Legros did to not only save, but build the park, my main influence was from Bob (Munger), and his style, drive and desire certainly was influenced by Roose and Legros."

In their definitive book on the resort, *Cedar Point, The Queen of American Watering Places*, authors David and Diane Francis tied everything together. "Schneider, Roose, Legros, Munger and Kinzel could be considered descendants of the astute George A. Boeckling. Like him, they saw in Cedar Point the potential for something more than a run-of-the-mill amusement park. They envisioned a truly great family entertainment facility. An amusement park, yes, but more than that, a place of beautiful white sandy beaches and luxury hotels and first class restaurants. A true summer resort in every sense of the word – with something for people of all ages."

The Cedar Point Boardwalk in the 1930s. The slogan for the Cyclone coaster in the background was "scientifically built for speed, thrills and safety." (Photo Courtesy of the Rutherford B. Hayes Presidential Center, Charles E. Frohman Collection.)

One of the first things Roose and Legros did when they purchased the park was to upgrade and expand the Cedar Point Marina, by that time one of the largest on Lake Erie. In 1999, Dick also expanded the Marina and today it is a major draw. People can dock for a fee and enjoy the park and the other amenities of the peninsula. Some stay all summer and enjoy their boats as their summer home, some stay for one day to enjoy the park or to dine at one of the restaurants.

Dick takes a rest during opening of Castaway Bay in 2004. (Cedar Point Photo)

Marketing VP Hildebrandt said Dick truly had the "creative spirit of the place. He challenged the organization to go in different directions and saw the opportunity to develop the resort side of the park." Hildebrandt's guest surveys showed that one-third of the park guests were from out of market and stayed in the Sandusky area while visiting the park. "Why not capture them and give them an opportunity to stay on our property, within walking distance of our attractions," surmised Dick.

In a 1990 interview with *CEO Interview* magazine, Dick reiterated the importance of having in-park lodging. "I would say the biggest growth area, purely from a percentage standpoint would be the accommodations division." In a later talk with *Amusement Business*, Dick pointed out that getting back to the park's resort roots is important for growth and that it isn't expensive or difficult. "If the tourist traffic is already established the only true cost is the building of the facilities. Most of the (operating) costs are already in place. Our marketing and sales departments are established. Food service is already here and our retail program is already in place. The synergies are here and there isn't a lot of overlap in operating costs."

A family resort needs a variety of options to make it a viable destination. Under Dick's leadership, Cedar Point added Soak City Waterpark (1988), with several additions including the $4.3 million doubling of the park in 1995 and a new wave pool in 1997; and Challenge Park (1992) which includes a two-acre Grand Prix raceway and a thirty-six hole miniature golf course. Three hotels were created: Sandcastle Suites (1990), with an additional ninety-one rooms added in 1992; the $10 million Breakers East, a new wing to Hotel Breakers, with three hundred rooms and luxury suites (1995) and Breakers Tower, a 230-room addition to Hotel Breakers (1999); and the Radisson Harbour Inn (1997), which was transformed into Castaway Bay, a $22 million Caribbean-themed indoor waterpark resort in November 2004.

Building an indoor, 237-room, year-round waterpark resort was a simple decision for Dick. "As other similar projects came into Sandusky (Great Wolf Lodge, Kalahari Resort) it gave us an opportunity to compete for the business, both in the summer and during the winter." He also mentions that the evolving twelve-month school calendar provides big breaks for the kids during the time Cedar Point is not open. "It helps drive revenue over an entire twelve-month period."

Breakers Express opened on the causeway in 2000 and the following year, Lighthouse Point featuring cottages, cabins and RV campsites opened, centered around the old lighthouse, now the oldest building on the point.

In 2003, Dick worked with Hildebrandt, Lee Alexakos and their marketing team to initiate a plan to promote in markets outside the traditional three hundred mile primary area of Northern Ohio and Southern Michigan. A specially-funded test program to promote the entire package of the park, restaurants and hotels kicked off on Memorial Day of that year with full page advertisements in specific regional editions of *USA Today*. Research had identified the logical regions in which to promote – Baltimore, Washington D.C., Philadelphia, New York City, and Chicago. Throughout that season, the marketing team followed up the newspaper advertisements with radio ads and a heavy promotional schedule with media partners in each market. The campaign kicked off in conjunction with the opening of the record breaking Top Thrill Dragster coaster.

The park announced a $10 million capital program for 2004 with an emphasis on the resort side of the 364-acre park. With an occupancy rate of more than 90 percent, the park's accommodations were nearly booked solid during that summer, thanks in main part to the expanded marketing campaign.

The popular Cedar Point Marina, with the Mantis in the foreground.
(Cedar Point Photo)

Hildebrandt noted that "while we had always been a resort park, we were falling right into that trend of people looking for a two to three day getaway with an easy car trip of their home." Dick looks back and points out that while they kept adding accommodations, they kept getting filled up almost immediately. The market is still there and he thinks it will continue to grow. Today, the resort offers more than twelve-hundred hotel rooms, 156 cabins and ninety-seven luxury campsites on Lighthouse Point.

An important part of any resort package is the food and beverage offering. Dick and his food department addressed that issue both in the park and outside its gates by dishing up a wide variety of branded food opportunities that aren't commonly seen in a park setting. One of Dick's missions when he joined the park in 1972 as manager of food services was to build up the in-park department in order to phase out concessionaires and bring all food service in-house. He did so successfully then, but he went the other way in the 1990s and 2000s.

When the Radisson Harbour Hotel was purchased, it came with a franchised TGI Fridays, which also happened to be the number one highest grossing seasonal TGI Fridays, on a weekly basis, in the country. When Castaway Bay opened, the eatery did even better. Following the renovation of Hotel Breakers in 1999, Dick insisted that they add another TGI Fridays to that hotel instead of a planned buffet restaurant. The representative who came to look over the space couldn't understand why they would want to move the highly successful restaurant at Castaway Bay to another location. "I had to explain that we didn't want to move it, we wanted to expand our franchise and build another," Dick said. It was built and within two years, they were told the TGI Fridays inside Hotel Breakers was the highest grossing seasonal operation in the country on a weekly basis, and the one at Castaway Bay was number three.

A Perkins franchise was also added to the hotel and is packed most of the time. Inside the park, national franchises were added during Dick's oversight. He first saw the Johnny Rocket's hamburger diner at Opry Mills in Nashville and immediately envisioned it inside the park on the site of the Fascination parlor. It became only the third Johnny Rockets in the state of Ohio. Pink's Hot Dogs, Starbucks, Panda Express, and several well-known local brands, including Toft's ice cream, Quaker Steak & Lube (which replaced TGI Fridays at Castaway Bay in 2015), Famous Dave's BBQ and Tomo Hibachi Grill are also doing well, all being offered as part of the overall Cedar Point experience.

Even though the resort is open only 120-plus days a year, it was required to purchase a standard franchise on all these and the park was required to follow all franchise rules and regulations except that it was permitted to charge a higher price and serve a more limited menu, similar to what franchises do at airports. The park is also required to pay the same marketing fees as do the other franchised locations, even though they are mostly available only to park guests.

Dick thought then, and still thinks that it makes sense to have a recognized food brand available in addition to the park's own outlets because people trust brand names. "When they walk into a branded restaurant, they know what they are going to get and that's an important thing for many people," Dick said. "Over the season, we had a captive audience of more than three million strong who wanted to eat a good meal at the park. It made sense to provide a wide choice for them."

The franchise concept works at Cedar Point, but Dick says it wouldn't at most other parks because of the high volume of guests here. "Our daily numbers at Cedar Point (including the park, marina, hotels and campgrounds) would average twenty-five thousand to thirty-five thousand people who wanted to eat one, maybe two meals, so we had the volume to support a national franchise."

Live Entertainment

To add diversity to the offerings of a resort, another important element is live entertainment, something Dick did not spend a great deal of time worrying about. He had confidence in the team in charge to present a good selection of live entertainment and he mostly stayed out of their way because "they certainly knew more about song and dance than I did."

He offered suggestions only on occasion and usually not about an existing show, but about a particular show concept.

"I was around for a long time and I felt I knew what the public wanted, so if something didn't look or sound right, only then would I question it." His idea of a good show was simple. "As long as the guests seem to be enjoying it and as long as the costumes were neat and clean and there were no runs in the lady's nylons, I was fine with the show."

While at Valleyfair, Dick brought in a laser light show that was performed just before closing time each night and it helped keep guests in the park longer and later, which translated to more food and beverage sales. When he returned to Cedar Point, he started a similar nighttime presentation and it has grown larger and more spectacular each year. The colorful, upbeat show with music, lasers and pyrotechnics is "a great way to close things down for the day. People leave on a happy note."

Historic Preservation

When he took over the company, Dick inherited an historic park. Through the years he needed to keep a delicate balance and in some cases he was damned if he did and damned if he didn't. How to deal with the Hotel Breakers in 1999 was probably his biggest dilemma.

As management was getting serious about promoting Cedar Point as a resort destination, Hotel Breakers was looked upon as somewhat of a white elephant. It was a six hundred room hotel that was in bad shape and if it were to be a viable part of the resort and be bookable, it needed to be modernized. People aren't coming to a hotel where the rooms aren't air conditioned and the toilets are down the hall. What needed to be done wasn't necessarily in step with the demands of the historic lists the hotel was on. The park ended up with a contemporary, workable hotel all while trying to keep as much of its historic charm as possible. The 1999 addition was just one of the upgrades Hotel Breaker experienced. It has been updated, renovated and added onto many times since its opening in 1905, the latest for the 2015 season.

It was mostly the locals who raised an uproar over the renovation of the hotel that eventually caused it to lose its historic status. "They ended up liking what we did and felt it was a great improvement, but they were sad it had lost the historic designation."

Ever mindful of the park's rich history, management over the past forty years has tried to preserve as much of the old resort as possible. The de-commissioned 1862 lighthouse has been preserved and now serves as storage, and the old iron streetlamps that once lit the way through the resort, are now used to hang colorful flower baskets each summer.

Dick and his team take great pride in the $100,000 restoration of the Coliseum, built in 1906, which houses the historic ballroom on the second floor and an expansive arcade on the ground level. It was in the ballroom, once touted as the "Largest Dancing Pavilion on the Great Lakes," and frequented by the likes of John Philip Sousa, Duke Ellington, Benny Goodman, Louis Armstrong and most of the other big bands of the day, that Dick's big retirement gala was held on Sept. 10, 2011.

Dick at IAAPA Convention with his friends Gasper Lococo, center, and Joe Meck. (Tim O'Brien Photo)

Complete with big band entertainment and nearly four hundred guests, the historical significance of the evening's setting "is particularly appropriate considering Dick Kinzel's contributions to Cedar Fair and the amusement park industry are both inspirational and long lasting," read the introduction to the evening's program. That night with all the accolades and happy toasts about his career was a humbling experience for Dick. "I knew they were planning a party for me but I had no idea it was going to be anything like it turned out to be. I especially liked that it was held at the park in one of our oldest structures. It was quite an honor."

Gasper Lococo, a man who Dick identifies as a mentor, attended the gala evening. Dick met Lococo at a restaurant supply store in Cleveland in 1973 and they have been friends ever since. Lococo, a former Cedar Point executive, left in 1969, along with several others from the park and purchased Geauga Lake Amusement Park, near Cleveland, which Dick would eventually have in his stable of parks from 2004 to 2007.

"I met Gasper before I left Cedar Point for Valleyfair and he was a very knowledgeable park operator who graciously shared his knowledge with me over the years." When Dick would come back to Ohio, he would make it a point to visit Geauga Lake and see what Lococo was doing. Dick said he learned a lot from his mentor. They both ran parks with less than a million in attendance and they shared many of the same problems. "I remember asking him for advice when we were getting ready to start a concert series at Valleyfair. The first thing he told me was to never book anyone if I had heard of them. That would mean the act was too old to appeal to our park's younger demographic and nobody would come. He was right!"

Dick and Judy at Dick's Gala Retirement Party. (Tim O'Brien Photo)

Lococo said Dick was always full of ideas and would share that excitement with him on those visits. "He is an upright individual. I was impressed because he was a risk taker and he stood up and fought for what he believed in." said Lococo. "He did all right for himself."

PART FOUR:
Dick's $2 Billion Spending Spree

The most fun Dick had while heading up Cedar Fair was the negotiating and the buying of other park properties. He would eventually buy ten amusement parks, two water parks, two hotel properties and one marina. In addition he built three waterparks and an indoor waterpark resort. Total cost of all these projects was nearly $2 billion.

Before Dick got control of the checkbook, two important acquisitions were completed that laid the groundwork for what Dick would purchase in the future. Northern Ohio businessmen George Roose and Emile Legros moved Cedar Point into the modern era when they purchased the entire 364-acre, seven mile long peninsula in 1957 for $350,000. In 1978, Bob Munger, as president and CEO, purchased Valleyfair for $15 million, creating the two-park company that would lead to the creation of Cedar Fair, the company Dick took over in 1986.

In a 1990 discussion with *CEO Interviews,* Dick pointed out that the company, then with two parks, is "at the stage where we would like to expand our business by adding another park," and then added the caveat that "we are a very conservative company and we wouldn't buy a property if we were uncomfortable with the risk." He stressed that the most likely way to grow would be through external growth. "As far as building a new park, that would be unlikely for us because it's just so costly. If we are going to grow, it would be by acquisition and we would probably stay in our industry."

Staying and growing within the industry he knew best, gave Dick and his team a targeted approach toward the key objective. He told a reporter with the *Cleveland Enterprise* in 1994 (three years before buying Knott's Berry Farm, a year-round park) that they would need to stay with what they knew. "This is the only business we're in .... We do one thing. We run amusement parks and we only have 130 or so days each year to make money. When the parks shut down, that's it and if you've had a bad season, you have to wait until next year to correct it. Management is quite focused and I think all of us eat, sleep and dream about the parks."

While many Cedar Fair investors wanted the conservative company to be more growth oriented, Dick and his team were careful to protect the investment. "Being conservative, I always concentrated on maintaining and protecting the cash distribution (to unit holders) and unless something can be accretive within the first year or two, we're just not comfortable acquiring it." Dick is a hard ride park type of guy and prefers coasters over waterparks for several reasons. "The margins are better at a ride park. You have more attendance and you have a better per-capita spending." But with that said, his acquisition strategy included waterparks if the right opportunity presented itself, and especially if that opportunity was near an existing Cedar Fair ride park, where operational synergies would work best.

Dick's first purchase was Dorney Park & Wildwater Kingdom in Allentown, Pa., in 1992 which had its own in-park waterpark and his next was the two-park complex of Worlds of Fun/Oceans of Fun in Kansas City, Mo. Later, in Southern California, he would buy two stand-alone waterparks and build another from scratch next to Knott's Berry Farm.

The Dorney Deal

"A diamond in the rough" is how Dick described Dorney Park when he first looked at it as a potential acquisition target. That's why he bought it. Even though it was in a very competitive market, Dick felt if he added rides and incorporated the company's proven management and marketing techniques, it could make a significant contribution to the bottom line. The park was in rough shape and several other companies had looked at it and passed.

It was a bumpy start. The deal to buy Dorney Park was announced on Jan. 23, 1992; the deal died on April 27; it came back to life on May 25; the deal was finalized on July 21; and Cedar Fair took over on July 22. The holdup was a forty-one acre plot of land adjacent to the park. It was owned by the township who wanted initially to lease it to Cedar Fair for $4,300 an acre per year, with height and use restrictions. Dick wanted to own it without any restrictions and offered the town commissioners $70,200 per acre. They countered with $84,348. Cedar Fair walked away and it looked like the deal was dead. The agreement to purchase the park was contingent on acquiring those acres, which Cedar Fair wanted for parking and future expansion. It was important to own that land with no restrictions.

At Dorney Park's closing, Dick poses with Harris Weinstein, left, and park GM Bill Near. (Cedar Point Photo)

Negotiations resumed and Cedar Fair ended up buying the land for $77,000 an acre, with the principal owner of

Dorney, Harris Weinstein contributing $812,000 toward the deal. There were no restrictions in the final deal. With the purchase, Cedar Fair began to tap into the big Eastern U.S. market, more than doubling its marketing area, going from thirty million to seventy million potential customers.

The purchase price consisted of approximately $21 million of limited partnership units and the assumption of approximately $27 million of long-term debt. It was Dick's first negotiation and while he enjoyed it, he claims it was one of the longest and most complicated ordeals he would ever experience.

Within a couple years, the units Weinstein had received for the deal had grown in value, substantially increasing his final take for the park. During the annual parks convention in Orlando several years after the transaction, Dick ran into Weinstein who greeted him with a big smile and a hug. "He said he should create a statue of me and put it in his back yard," Dick said. "He said Cedar Fair made him a very rich man."

Bill Near, Dick's former boss at Cedar Point and the man who hired him in 1972, was named Dorney's VP and general manager. It was announced that Cedar Fair would invest between $15 million and $25 million in the park for the 1993 season.

Dorney had four coasters in operation when Cedar Fair purchased the park and Dick spearheaded the addition of six more over the years, including the junior coasters. One of the coasters that came with the park was a wooden giant named Hercules, which Dick described as "the roughest roller coaster ride in the world." Even rougher than Cedar Point's Mean Streak.

Built in 1989, the ride was heralded as the tallest wooden coaster in the world which immediately got the park into trouble in a very public battle with Six Flags who claimed they had the tallest. By the time it was torn down following the 2003 season, it was the least ridden coaster in the park. It was a maintenance headache and Dick said it was a money pit to keep running. A couple years after purchasing the park, Cedar Fair took Weinstein to court over the problems with Hercules, an action which Dick said was "a dumb mistake" on his part. They sued the former owner stating that he knew the coaster had problems and he should have told Cedar Fair it was a bad coaster. Weinstein countered noting that Cedar Fair was the roller coaster expert and they should have KNOWN it was a bad coaster. "He was right, the suit was thrown out."

Dick realized in 1992 that he would not be able to act both as the president and CEO as well as the general manager of Cedar Point. Shortly after Near was named general manager at Dorney, Don Miears, who had served twenty-three years with Cedar Point, was appointed Executive VP and general manager of Cedar Point. Walt Wittmer, who had served as Dick's VP of Maintenance at Valleyfair, had been named VP and general manager of that park when Dick returned to Ohio in 1986. All three general managers reported directly to Dick.

Miears says he was "floored" when Dick called him into the office to tell him about his promotion. "I didn't expect or anticipate it but I gladly accepted it." Miears said it was an easy transition taking the general manager job over from Dick "because the place was already a really, really good park. It wasn't broken so I didn't have to fix anything." Miears was also elected to the Board of Directors in 1993.

A Worldly Deal

The deal to acquire Worlds of Fun/Oceans of Fun parks in Kansas City, Mo., was finalized on July 28, 1995 in a transaction valued at $40 million. The price consisted of the assumption of approximately $17 million in debt and the issuance of approximately $22.2 million in Cedar Fair units. Dan Keller, senior VP of operations under Dick at Cedar

Point, was named VP and general manager of the park. Fresh out of college, Keller was the first person Dick hired in 1973.

"Worlds of Fun is an exceptionally beautiful park with more theming than at our other parks," said Dick at the time of the purchase. The park is themed around Jules Verne's adventure book, *Around the World in Eighty Days* and on the day Cedar Fair acquired it, the park had three roller coasters, including Timber Wolf, which had been consistently rated as one of the Top Ten wooden coasters since its opening in 1989.

The negotiation was much easier than the one with Dorney Park three years earlier. Worlds of Fun was represented at the table by Lee Derrough, the president of the park which was owned by Lamar Hunt, the owner of the NFL's Kansas City Chiefs. Dick recalls that dealing with both of them was a pleasure and that Hunt is "one of the nicest people I have ever met." He was also impressed with Derrough, who served on the Cedar Fair board for ten years following the acquisition.

"I met Lamar after the deal was done. Great guy! He invited Judy and me to a couple of Kansas City Chiefs football games in Kansas City, and then we joined him in Cleveland, in the visiting team's owner's box, to watch a Browns game."

Dick immediately started thinking big steel for the park and in 1998 the first coaster he added was the 205-foot tall Mamba. He was especially excited about the Oceans of Fun side of the complex, at the time, the largest waterpark in the Midwest. He called it a "first class operation that had a great diversity of rides, slides and attractions."

By 1996, the world-wide frenzy of small family-owned parks being bought up by larger park companies was in full swing. Cedar Fair owned and operated four parks and a couple of waterparks and would be adding Knott's Berry Farm the following year. *Amusement Business* asked Dick if the disappearance of the mom and pop parks was a bad thing for the industry as a whole.

"It isn't bad. It takes a great deal of resources to keep parks competitive and alive these days and many small operators can't keep up. Park chains have deep pockets and can benefit from the synergies from their other parks. Corporate ownership is part of the current evolution of the American amusement park. It's here, and it's good for the industry as a whole."

His philosophy on running a group of parks? He keeps the parks as much of a mom and pop operation as possible and treats them more as a collection of parks instead of a chain of parks. He thinks the typical park guest rarely notices or cares who owns the park as long as it lives up to his or her expectations.

He noted that he always left it up to the general managers to run the parks, although there were some corporate procedures that had to be followed in several areas such as safety. Other than that, each general manager did his or her own thing and wasn't bothered by corporate as long as the numbers supported them.

Acquiring the First Year-Round Park

In early 1997, the family-owned Knott's Berry Farm in Buena Park, Calif., engaged the investment banking firm of Goldman Sachs & Co. to help identify a strategic partner to assist in the growth or the outright sale of the park. That led to Dick sitting down at the table to negotiate. This was a pretty simple acquisition with no last minute surprises. It was down to just a few other bidders. "We had put in a bid and we had to put in an additional $10 million and we got it." The deal was finalized on Dec. 29, 1997 and was valued at approximately $245 million, consisting of the issuance of

Dick was Grand Marshal of the Buena Park, Calif. Silverado Days shortly after acquiring Knott's Berry Farm. Judy shared the stage coach during the parade.

$150 million of limited partnership units and the payment of approximately $94 million in cash, borrowed from Cedar Fair's revolving credit agreement.

The issuance of approximately six million units was divided between the thirteen Knott's family members who owned the park. The transaction gave the family a twelve percent ownership position in Cedar Fair. Unit transactions had been previously instrumental in acquiring both Dorney Park and Worlds of Fun and would be important in acquiring Michigan's Adventure in 2001. Exchanging units for the properties made sense to Dick and his board. By doing so, Cedar Fair did not have to borrow all the funds needed for an acquisition.

Each unit could go down and the seller would lose some of the purchase value, or it could go up and they would end up getting more of a value from their park, as it did in the case of Dorney Park. Units instead of cash also had a tax benefit for the seller and the cash distribution from the units each year was an added benefit. By accepting units as payment, the sellers showed trust that Dick and Cedar Fair would continue to do well.

Included in the deal with Knott's, Cedar Fair acquired the licensing rights for the Peanuts characters and the management contract for Knott's Camp Snoopy, a seven-acre indoor park at Mall of America in Bloomington, Minn. The Peanuts characters had been a part of Knott's for seventeen years and today are a major theming element in the children's areas of all Cedar Fair parks.

Unlike a lot of cartoon characters, the Peanuts gang is known and loved by all age groups. Snoopy dolls, Charlie Brown t-shirts, and Woodstock stuffed toys are seen everywhere in the parks. Dick throws in one of his favorite words here. "Marketable." Peanuts characters are very marketable.

Shortly after acquiring the rights and bringing the characters to Cedar Point, John Hildebrandt worked out a deal with the hospitals in the area to present a Snoopy doll to all newborns. "They are packaged up nicely, and of course our logo is on each one. Often, Snoopy is the child's first toy," said Dick.

Cedar Fair's management contract ended at Mall of America in March 2005 and negotiations regarding the mall's use of the Peanuts characters continued through January 2006. Those talks were unsuccessful and the characters were pulled out of the park. The re-theming of everything Peanuts took place and the name was changed to The Park at Mall of America. The mall owners managed the "generic" park until it became a Nickelodeon-themed attraction in March 2008, which it remains today.

The following December, the first wooden coaster at Knott's Berry Farm, the $24 million Custom Coasters Int. GhostRider opened to rave reviews. The park's VP and general manager Jack Falfas, who had been appointed to this position from his VP of operations job at Cedar Point, was quite aware of the potential of the GhostRider. While neither he nor Dick had anything to do with designing or the purchasing of the ride, they were both delighted to find that it was in the pipeline and under construction when they acquired the park.

GhostRider opened on Dec. 8, 1998 and Falfas told the media that it immediately boosted park attendance by double digits. Dick said he knew he had a winner when coaster enthusiasts started chatting about it on the Internet. A large number of enthusiasts from around the country took advantage of it opening during the holidays, to visit and experience it.

The park had seven operating coasters when Cedar Fair took over and including the GhostRider, six more were added prior to 2012.

With an eye for making Knott's as much of a destination resort as space would allow, Cedar Fair purchased the adjacent Buena Park Hotel in February 1999 for $17.5 million in cash and immediately spent another $10 million in renovating the entire property. It reopened in early 2000 as the Radisson Resort Knott's Berry Farm hotel, making it the 400th Radisson property in the world. Noting that the park was then able to offer guests all the elements of a full vacation destination, Dick was happy with the potential of the 320 room hotel. He said it made a lot of sense to acquire and upgrade the property. It was on the same plot of land as the amusement park and was directly adjacent to the park. Owning the hotel, Dick said, gave them the ability to control the destiny of that property.

In October 1999 Cedar Fair stepped outside its regular acquisition course and purchased its first stand-alone waterpark. White Water Canyon in Chula Vista, Calif. was located halfway between San Diego and Mexico and two hours south of Buena Park. The opportunity to purchase it "just fell into our lap" Dick said. The cash purchase price was $11.6 million. Opened in 1997, the thirty-three acre park never made much of an impression and had very little brand recognition even in its own market. The plan Dick and his team came up with was to rebrand it with a 1950s California beach town theme and to capitalize on the strength of the Knott's name in Southern California. They renamed it Knott's Soak City U.S.A.

The following June, the $25 million, thirteen acre Knott's Soak City U.S.A., directly adjacent to the park in Buena Park, opened as the theme park's second gate, requiring separate admission. It too had a theme that paid homage to Southern California's famous surf beaches. While small in acreage, the park opened with twenty-two water adventures including sixteen high speed thrill slides and a wave pool with a large sun bathing deck.

With a common name, the two Soak City properties kicked off a unified marketing and promotional campaign that was communicated throughout Southern California. Dick said the first season at both parks was "very successful and unexpectedly profitable."

Oasis Water Park was brought into the Soak City family in May 2001. The sixteen acre seasonal waterpark in Palm Springs, Calif., was acquired for $9.1 million cash purchase and rebranded as Soak City U.S.A. Palm Springs. Dick said when the opportunity to buy Oasis presented itself, he saw it as a solid opportunity to expand the Soak City brand even further in Southern California. The three waterparks were to be "operated and marketed in tandem," a news release at the time noted.

During the first season the park was renamed Knott's Oasis Water Park and most of the efforts were put into safety training and infrastructure upgrades. The $2 million transformation to the Southern California beach theme started after the park closed for the season. In 2002, the first full season under the Soak City U.S.A. banner, the Palm Springs property hit what the marketing director of the park called a home run. The season pass cost was lowered and marketing was expanded resulting in a 40 percent increase in both revenue and attendance. Geographically located in a triangle, the three Soak City parks were approximately two hours from each other. One season pass allowed access to all three.

A great deal of money saving synergies were realized by treating the three Soak City waterparks as a division and not as individual parks, according to Dick. Since all three were seasonal and run with the assistance of the Knott's Berry Farm management team, a minimum number of employees were needed. Additional savings were realized in nearly every operating category. "With all of these synergies, we were able to make the parks work while the previous owners, who each owned only that one park, could not."

While the Soak City adjacent to Knott's Berry Farm is still in the Cedar Fair family, the two others have been sold, both since Dick left the company. In November 2012, Sea World Parks & Entertainment purchased the Chula Vista property and renamed it Aquatica. In August 2013, CNL Lifestyle Properties purchased the Palm Springs property for $8.7 million and renamed it Wet 'n' Wild Palm Springs prior to the 2014 season.

The one acquisition that got away, or more likely thrown away by Dick was in 2000. With his management team already in place at the park, he pulled the plug on a deal with Visionland, in Bessemer, Ala., near Birmingham, only a few weeks before the season was to begin. Dick had negotiated a five year management deal with an option to buy, but he soon became "uncomfortable" with the deal and the situation when he couldn't get any answers or would get the "wrong" answer to a bevy of questions. A "round peg in a square hole" is how Dick explained the feelings that made him pull out of the deal.

Management Strength

Many times when big parks gobble up smaller parks, the team sent from the bigger park doesn't have the skills to operate the new property. Cedar Fair, according to Dick, never had that problem. In fact, he said management depth was always his team's biggest strength. Most of his management pool had started out as seasonal help and they knew that long, hot hours were needed to get the job done. The younger management team knew company procedures and policies and was ready and prepared to accept new challenges, which, according to Dick, freed up Cedar Fair to acquire more properties.

He saw summer employment at the parks as a type of a farm system for future management stock. Veteran management got the opportunity to get a good look at the kids summer after summer and if he or another member of the management team especially liked someone, they would try to recruit them for full time employment. Although he never worked part-time at the park, Dick feels he was a part of that farm system himself and he's proud of his fellow workers who have gone on to bigger things. Everywhere you look in this industry, chances are you'll find someone who got his or her training at Cedar Point.

In wanting to protect the Michigan and Detroit markets from Chicago's Six Flags Great America, Cedar Fair officials had aspirations to build a new park in Michigan for decades. In 1973, before the Valleyfair acquisition, Cedar Point announced that it was building a park on the four hundred acres of land it owned in Irish Hills, just outside Detroit. Environmental issues killed that deal. Two years later, the company tried again, this time on an abandoned military base in Battle Creek. For various reasons that deal fell through as well. While the need to keep someone from building a park between Cedar Point and Chicago was still there, nothing more was done to make it happen until 2001. Michigan's Adventure in Muskegon came on the market and Cedar Fair acquired it for approximately $28 million in Cedar Fair units.

It was and remains today, the smallest Cedar Fair amusement park in both attendance and revenues. To make it more attractive to Michigan residents, the $90 season pass was good not only at Michigan's Adventure but also at Cedar Point and all the other Cedar Fair parks. "Why go to Six Flags and pay if I already have a pass to get into ALL Cedar Fair parks," was the concept behind the marketing ploy.

Michigan's Adventure had already opened for the 2001 season when Cedar Fair completed the purchase and as such, the only capital investment made that year was in landscaping and infrastructure work that continued into 2002. The two wooden coasters, Wolverine Wildcat and Shivering Timbers, were still a big draw and Dick didn't feel another coaster was needed at that time. The park had six coasters and in 2008, Thunderhawk, an inverted Vekoma coaster was moved here from Geauga Lake. More than $5 million was spent in 2002, featuring seven new rides including a hydro-flume raft slide and several other family and kid's ride. A Peanuts-themed live show was added featuring Snoopy, Charlie Brown and other costumed characters.

Dick liked dealing with Roger Jourdan, who owned Michigan's Adventure. They had everything negotiated and were down to the last minute when Dick realized that the property across the street from the park that was part of the deal, contained huge piles of stone that the county wanted removed as soon as possible. Neither Roger nor Dick wanted the stone and it was going to be expensive to haul it out. Roger had been in the stone business and that's why the excess stone was there. "When I found out that it had to be removed, and much to the disapproval of the attorneys in the room, Roger and I went out into the hall to discuss the stones removal. The talk had gone on for hours across the table, so we thought we should discuss it privately." This is how Dick recalls the conversation: "Roger, I don't even have a truck and you do. How am I going to get rid of all that stone?" Roger looked at Dick and said: "You're right, I have the trucks." Dick said they shook on it and within a few minutes the deal was signed.

Dick threw out the ceremonial first pitch for his favorite baseball team, the Cleveland Indians in 2001.
(Jason Werling Photos)

The terrorist attacks on Sept. 11, 2001 took place early on a Tuesday morning during the fall shoulder season when all the Cedar Fair seasonal parks were closed. Knott's closed for the day, but when it opened the following morning, it did little business and had only sparse crowds for the rest of the week. The seasonal parks opened as scheduled later that week and did good business. Those parks are all drive-to parks and people didn't have to worry about air travel to get there. By the weekend, a lot of people were looking for a diversion and attendance was on or above daily projections.

The IAAPA Summer Manager's Meeting was set to commence on Sept. 13 at Cedar Point but was immediately cancelled. Nearly three hundred park executives from around the world who were registered, would not have been able get there due to flight cancellations. Some who came in early, were not able to leave, so Dick and Judy were hosts to about twenty-five people until they could catch planes to leave, some a week later.

The tent, food and beverages had already been ordered for the function and couldn't be returned, so the group ate and drank their way through the week. Dick recalls those days with a smile noting that the situation brought together an "amazing bunch of people. That was a week I will always remember."

Something else Dick remembers is how clear the sky was, how void of jet contrails, something he always saw in the sky from the beach in front of his house. "I remember standing out there one night that week looking up at an amazingly clear sky and thinking that it was the same sky our forefathers saw one hundred years before. It was an amazing feeling."

The confab was cancelled totally that year, but IAAPA officials moved the schedule around and selected to hold it at Cedar Point the following year, 2002. Dick was ecstatic that he would be able to host the prestigious group, even though it was a year later than planned. It was a lot easier to plan for it the second time he said. "We dusted off the program from the year before, made a few tweaks and we were ready."

Protecting the Eastern Front

To further protect Cedar Point's Eastern front from the East coast parks and to eliminate its closest competitor, Cedar Fair finalized its acquisition of Six Flags Worlds of Adventure on April 8 only three weeks prior to its opening for the 2004 season. The cash transaction was valued at $145 million. The park, founded in 1887, operated as Geauga Lake until 2000 when it was flagged as Six Flags Ohio, following the Premier Park (its owner since 1995) purchase of the Six Flags chain. In early 2001, Six Flags additionally bought the adjacent SeaWorld of Ohio, combined the two, and renamed it Six Flags Worlds of Adventure, offering both parks for one ticket.

With the marketing advantage of being a Six Flags park, many thought early on that Geauga Lake would give Cedar Point, its nearest competitor, a run for its money. In a story entitled "Will Six Flags overpower Cedar Point?" reporter Beth Naser had a little fun in setting the tone of her story. "The fur will fly this spring when Snoopy and Bugs Bunny go head-to-head in the battle of the amusement park giants." Six Flags immediately added four new coasters increasing their coaster count to ten to be more competitive with its Cedar Point rival. It didn't take long for Six Flags to realize they could not compete nor could they make the park work after several years of trying and were more than happy to sell it.

Dick, Jack Falfas, left, and Lee Jewett celebrating the grand opening of the "new" Geauga Lake in 2004.

The park, located only eighty-five miles from Cedar Point was quickly re-branded back to Geauga Lake in 2004. Six Flags kept the killer whale and a few other marine animals and Cedar Fair donated the rest to various zoos across the country. "With PETA and other animal activist groups being the way they are, I didn't need the added aggravation of marine animals in our parks." That was not a new revelation by Dick. By the early 1990s he had closed down Cedar Point's aquarium and the live dolphin show that Munger had created many years earlier.

SeaWorld Ohio was averaging about 1.3 million in attendance and Six Flags Ohio was around 1.7 million. With the two combined, Six Flags Worlds of Adventure could not get back to that three million mark. The decreased overall attendance, plus the fact that only one admission fee was being collected for the two parks, didn't make financial sense. Six Flags couldn't make it work and as it turned out, Cedar Fair couldn't make it work. Some people to this day think Dick bought it only to close it down, but he insists that's not the case.

By the end of the 2007 season, it was evident that Geauga Lake and its new Wildwater Kingdom waterpark were not going to be money makers for the company and it was announced on Sept. 21, 2007 that the historic Geauga Lake park would not open again the following spring. The $25 million, thirty acre Wildwater Kingdom, which had been

Cedar Fair closes Geauga Lake
Waterpark will remain open

The closing of Geauga Lake was front page headlines, as shown here from the *Sandusky Register*.

built over a two year period on the SeaWorld side of the property remained open and is still operated as a stand-alone waterpark by Cedar Fair today. "We were taking it year by year. In 2004 we had sold the board on a three-year turnaround and going into 2007, our fourth year, we were certainly behind the curve."

It was a hard decision for Dick to close that park. No one likes to admit they can't make something work. "It was just so big. We kept throwing dollar after dollar at it." After closing Geauga Lake, the Cedar Fair family had eleven parks and management made good use of what they could from the now-closed park. Five of the Geauga Lake roller coasters and many of the smaller rides were distributed between the various Cedar Fair parks. "We tried very hard to utilize anything and everything we could. I didn't want to see things wasted."

It wouldn't have made sense for Dick to sell Geauga Lake as an operating park, in essence creating additional competition to Cedar Point. The land which is now for sale has the covenant that whoever buys it cannot put any rides on the property, ever.

Ironically, what eventually kept attendance from growing at Geauga Lake was the strength of its nearest competition – Cedar Point. "We got beat by ourselves," Dick said. Gasper Lococo, the former owner of Geauga Lake and Dick's longtime friend looks back and thinks Cedar Fair could have made the park work if they would have given it more time and invested more money.

A year after Cedar Fair bought the Ohio property, in August 2005, Six Flags corporate put up a "for sale" sign on its thirty remaining US, Canadian and Mexican parks. Rumors began quickly that Cedar Fair was negotiating to buy the entire group. Adding credence to the rumor was the fact that Cedar Fair had purchased the Ohio Six Flags park only months earlier. "No, we did not make a play for Six Flags at that time," notes Dick adding he had talked with the park chain earlier in the 2000s. "I was always searching for good acquisitions and yes, we had talks with Kieran Burke, the head of Six Flags, on a couple occasions and discussed everything from potentially merging our companies to an outright purchase. But nothing ever came out of those preliminary discussions."

Premier Parks $965 million purchase of the Six Flags chain in 1998 did not initially include the two original Six Flags parks – Six Flags Over Georgia in Atlanta or Six Flags Over Texas in Dallas, both of which were managed by Six Flags corporate but owned by different partnerships.

Dick went to Dallas to talk with the ownership partners to see if it would be a good fit for Cedar Fair and to talk about potentially buying that property. Once the meeting started, the partners who owned the park kept adding on one thing after another that they wanted and Dick immediately saw what was happening. "It was obvious to me that Six Flags corporate would end up with both the Dallas and Atlanta properties. The partnerships were just testing the waters with us in an attempt to show that there was interest in the parks and at the same time raise the final price that Six Flags would end up paying." He was right. Both parks went back to Six Flags corporate. Dick never regretted that trip to Dallas "because it gave us the opportunity see the financials, if nothing else."

Will SpongeBob be Saved?

Actually no, SpongeBob got canned, but more on that later.

The biggest purchase Dick made during his reign surprised almost everyone. In a stunning move, Dick and his right hand man Jack Falfas and Cedar Fair's chief financial officer Peter Crage negotiated a $1.24 billion buyout of the five Paramount Parks. It was a huge acquisition. It would nearly double Cedar Fair's revenue and attendance in just one season.

Kings Island, one of the Paramount Parks near Cincinnati, had been on Dick's "want list" for more than a decade. In the early 1990s, before the park was sold to Paramount, Dick had been in negotiations with Carl Lindner, chairman of American Financial Corporation, then owner of Kings Island. As they pursued a potential sale, a tax problem surfaced and when they couldn't work around it, the deal was left on the table. Upon Paramount's purchase of the park in 1992, Dick let it be known that if they were ever going to sell, he would be interested. When the rumors started flying that Paramount's corporate owner, CBS, wanted to divest itself of the five parks, Dick jumped in and ended up as one of the four finalists and the eventual top bidder.

On May 22, 2006 when the news came out that Cedar Fair was buying the parks, but before a lot of the details were known, questions about unit prices and cash distribution were being raised. Dick told investors and analysts during a conference call at the time to "have confidence in us. Have patience. It's going to take some time (to figure out all the specific details)." He noted that the five parks were quality properties that were built well and had been maintained. Unlike previous acquisitions, Cedar Fair won't have to "go in and rebuild them" he told the investors and analysts.

The purchase turned out to be one of the largest deals ever made in amusement park history. The Toledo *Blade* shared the news on its front page, May 23, 2006.

One of Dick's quotes in the official Cedar Fair press release, was picked up by most media around the country. "It is not every day that we have the chance to purchase five great family oriented parks that fit extremely well with our existing parks. It will add significant geographic diversity to our portfolio and improve our position as one of the largest regional amusement park operators in the world."

All five Paramount Parks were in different markets than existing Cedar Fair properties and in buying them, Cedar Fair did not duplicate or put in harm any of its legacy properties. In addition to Ohio's Kings Island, the purchase included Carowinds, in Charlotte, N.C.; Kings Dominion, near Richmond, Va.: Canada's Wonderland, near Toronto; and California's Great America in Santa Clara.

In addition to the parks, the deal included Star Trek: The Experience in Las Vegas and the management contract for Bonfante Gardens in Gilroy, Calif.

With a few changes, the interactive walk-through attraction, Star Trek, located in the Las Vegas Hilton became a good money maker for Cedar Fair, according to Dick, but Hilton had communicated that once the contract was up, the space was going to be used to expand the casino. Star Trek closed on Sept. 1, 2008. Bonfante Gardens opened in 2001 in Gilroy, Calif. and Paramount Parks took over the management in 2003. The park's name was changed to Gilroy Gardens in early 2007, shortly after Cedar Fair took over. The city of Gilroy purchased the park from the Bonfante family on March 5, 2008 and maintained Cedar Fair as its management company.

There were questions as to whether Cedar Fair would follow through on two specific projects underway that involved Paramount Parks. One was the building of a Great Wolf Lodge adjacent to Kings Island, and the other was a $625 million theme park development deal in Tianjin, China. "We rejected both of those projects. We wanted to stay focused on these five parks," Dick said.

With the inclusion of the Paramount Parks, Cedar Fair now owned four parks bringing in more than three million guests a year – Cedar Point, Knott's Berry Farm, Kings Island and Canada's Wonderland.

Cedar Point had always carried the weight and the responsibility for all the Cedar Fair parks, contributing a large part of the total revenue and nearly half of its cash flow. That model was a dangerous one and Dick felt diversification was needed as a safety net for the company. When he went to the board to discuss the Paramount acquisition, that need for diversity was a major selling point. He pointed out that while going into a billion dollars' worth of debt was risky, lacking diversity and lacking the opportunity to spread the risk around was even more of a danger. Once the eleven parks were assimilated, no one property contributed more than 22 percent of revenues.

In an interview with the *Plain Dealer* in Cleveland, industry veteran Dennis Speigel, president of Cincinnati-based International Theme Park Services was asked if the Paramount Park deal was a good one for Cedar Fair. "They got a wonderful group of parks, but they paid too much. At the time, the economy was different. Everybody was buoyant and excited. They thought they were doing the right thing." Speigel added that there was no major competition for the park properties and they got caught up in a bidding war.

Dick told *Amusement Today* that the night before he signed the documentation for the acquisition, he lost sleep, something he said he rarely did in all his years at the stressful top position. The fact that he never liked debt haunted him that night. "It dawned on me just how much one billion dollars is." He also told the same publication that he felt "energized" after the acquisition. "I am having more fun now than I have had in a long time."

A New Coaster Kingdom

Speigel pointed out in an interview with the *Cincinnati Enquirer* that upon the purchase, Cedar Fair became without a doubt, the dominant roller coaster operator in the world.

"No one else comes close," he said. Fifty-five coasters were operating that season at the five Paramount Parks and another forty-nine in the Cedar Fair legacy parks.

Dick Kinzel, the King of Roller Coasters, now reigned over more than one hundred scream machines, from coast to coast. Among that lot of coasters was the Beast at Kings Island, still Dick's favorite wooden coaster.

The acquisition of the five parks provided even more opportunities for Dick to flex his coaster muscles. During the decade prior to being purchased by Cedar Fair, Paramount Parks had put an emphasis on wooden coasters and family rides. "We felt if we were to grow those parks we had to put in more steel coasters to round out the appeal and provide more for the teens." Big steel it was.

It was an active period of new coaster construction and ride relocation from 2006 through the 2011 season. Even with the hundred plus coasters now in the Cedar Fair stable, Dick saw the need to create more. Several of the "new" coasters found at the parks during those years were moved from Geauga Lake, following the closing of that park at the close of the 2007 season.

At Kings Island, the X-Flight Flying Coaster from Vekoma was moved from Geauga Lake in 2007 and opened here as the Firehawk. In 2009 the $22 million, 230-foot tall B&M Diamondback was added.

In Canada's Wonderland, the $26 million, 230-foot tall B&M Behemoth debuted in 2008, followed by the premiere of the 306-foot tall $28 million B&M Leviathan in 2012.

Geauga Lake's B&M Dominator floorless coaster opened at Kings Dominion in 2008 and in 2010, Intamin's 305-foot tall, $25 million Intimidator 305 made its debut at the Richmond park.

Carowinds was the recipient of Geauga Lake's Headspin, a Vekoma Boomerang in 2009. It was renamed the Carolina Cobra. Also at Carowinds, the $23 million, 232-foot tall B&M Intimidator opened in 2010, followed by the $30 million

B&M Fury 325 that debuted in 2015 (the last coaster Dick had on his five-year plan when he retired).

No coasters were added to Great America during Dick's leadership, mostly because it was "not warranted" by attendance or revenue production. Great America was the least productive of the five Paramount Parks according to Dick.

Happy Coaster Fans

Coaster and thrill ride enthusiasts in Southern Ohio were quick to add their happiness to the news. They pointed out that Cedar Point concentrates on thrill rides while Kings Island focuses more on family attractions. Fans from the Southeast checked in with high hopes that more thrill rides would be added to their parks, Kings Dominion and Carowinds. Most of the Internet chatter approved of the deal, noting that Cedar Fair was a great park operator and they all felt the Paramount Parks would be in good hands.

Dick said the perception of the fans was correct. Cedar Fair had the reputation for being high thrill and Paramount's reputation was for great family entertainment. During the five years following the acquisition, Dick feels his team was able to blend thrills and coasters with family attractions to build strong properties that had something for all tastes.

Paramount Parks had strong licensing tie-ins with Nickelodeon to use the cable networks cartoon characters, such as SpongeBob and Dora the Explorer and others in the parks. They also had a deal with Hanna-Barbera for its characters, including Scooby-Doo. Of course, Cedar Fair owned the rights and had built very successful children's areas with the Peanuts gang. People wondered if Dick would mix the various cartoon characters into one big happy and colorful cartoon-filled children's area.

> **Dealing with the debt is top priority as Point's parent comes off a roller coaster year**
>
> # Cedar Fair's future

Cedar Fair's huge debt from the Paramount deal was big news for several years as seen here in a headline from the *Sandusky Register*.

There were still several years left on the character licensing deals and Dick initially wanted to keep them both. "We spent a lot of time talking and negotiating for both Nickelodeon and Hanna-Barbera licenses, but in the end it was going to be too expensive to keep them, plus Nickelodeon wanted complete creative control of their themed areas. That was something we weren't going to give up."

When asked in retrospect if he would buy the parks again, Dick didn't miss a beat. "Absolutely, it's a great fit and it was a lot of fun. Cedar Fair is much stronger today with those five parks."

He said there were no negative surprises and things went a lot smoother during the transition than any of his team imagined. The deal was announced in May and they did not take over until late June. During that time the transition teams were in place and all the management changes were mapped out. When the morning of the official turnover arrived "it went really, really smooth," he said at the time. Being mid-season, there weren't any immediate physical changes. To the park guest, it was still Paramount Kings Island or Paramount Canada's Wonderland. And once the Paramount name had been removed post season, Cedar Fair's name was not substituted. "No, outside of Sandusky, Ohio, the name Cedar Fair didn't mean a thing. We kept it simple. Great America, Kings Island, Kings Dominion, Canada's Wonderland and Carowinds – those are all well-known names, there was no need to tack on the owners name."

By the end of 2007, the first full season under Cedar Fair ownership, some of the changes made during the integration of the two park groups were raising their ugly heads, causing attendance drops at several of the Paramount Parks. Dick noted at the time that "this is mainly due to a drop in season pass attendance and the intentional reduction in the number of courtesy admissions in order to bring the parks more in line with our Cedar Fair pricing model." Long-time Paramount Park guests did not like some of the changes imposed on their parks. As a result, attendance at the five Paramount Parks declined 200,000 during the first season.

Cedar Fair parks had traditionally acquired 10 percent of their attendance from season passes and that number tallied nearly 40 percent at the Paramount Parks. Some of the season pass benefits were taken away knowing that some attendance would drop as a result, but not as much as it did. By the end of the season a new annual pass program was put in place and sales began to turn around.

Cedar Fair took over the Paramount Parks in June 2006 and combined attendance that year with the Cedar Fair parks was 12.7 million. In 2007, when all the parks were operated by Cedar Fair for the entire year, attendance grew to 19.3 million. During that first year, Dick noted that "overall we were pleased with our results as this has been a very busy and challenging year for the company." Talking about the 2007 results a year later, Dick said he was "pleased to report that 2007 was another very successful attendance year for the company," even with the attendance drop at the Paramount Parks. The integration of our new parks, he said, "continues to go well and we are where we expected to be on a combined basis at this point in the process."

A couple weeks before his retirement, Dick told Toledo *Blade* reporter Jon Chavez that history will prove in the end that the Paramount Park's purchase was his biggest achievement as CEO. "That's probably the thing I'm most proud of, making that acquisition."

The year before the acquisition, Dick had announced he would retire in 2007. However, when the negotiations with CBS became serious and it looked like Cedar Fair could end up with the parks, he assured the board of directors that if they wanted him to stay around for another three to five years to lead the integration of the new properties he would stay. They gave him a five-year extension.

Before officially dropping the Paramount Parks name from the five properties, Dick had talked with CBS about the idea of keeping the Paramount name on those five, plus adding it to the other Cedar Fair parks as well. The world came closer than it ever knew to having a Paramount's Dorney Park and a Paramount's Cedar Point. "When we bought those parks, we basically doubled the size of our company and we were just as much Paramount as Cedar Fair. We seriously considered using the Paramount name because of its marketing value, but it was going to cost us a great deal of money, so we stepped back." Today, Dick says he's glad that didn't happen. "It's not like we had a bad reputation and needed to change our names."

With so many properties however, Cedar Fair officials felt it was time to consider a name change. Cedar Fair now owned and operated eleven amusement parks, five outdoor waterparks, one indoor water park and six hotels in eight states and Canada. Dick noted a name change should be considered because "Cedar Fair L.P. didn't describe who we are or what we do." The company started calling itself Cedar Fair Entertainment Co. on Oct. 25, 2006. Legally they remained Cedar Point L.P., but from that date all business has been conducted using the new moniker.

PART FIVE:
After the Spending Spree

Dick's first year and the last couple years of his thirty-nine years with Cedar Point and Cedar Fair were not the best or the easiest, but "everything in the middle was great." The first year can be written off as a learning curve and by the time his second year began, Dick was on a roll that wouldn't stop for nearly four decades. During the last few years it was one discouraging and heart breaking thing after another. Some of what happed was deserved, most of it was just a matter of circumstances.

The amazing high Dick realized during his successful bid to purchase the Paramount Parks didn't last too long. He couldn't have known it at the time, but the debt incurred for that purchase, combined with several other money-related issues would plague him both personally and as CEO during the last several years of his career.

Personally, it all started on April 18, 2008, when he exercised an option to buy more than 650,000 Cedar Fair units at a price of $6.03 per unit. Units were trading at $22.90 at the time, giving his options a $14,885,000 market value. In order to acquire the units, Dick and his wife Judy borrowed, using a loan management account (LMA) of $7,681,482 from Merrill Lynch, using the new units as collateral with various funds, including Dick's salary, unit distribution and bonuses directed for payback. They never intended it to be a long-term loan. Merrill Lynch increased the maintenance requirement on the loan ten months later in March 2009. By that time, the Kinzels had paid back more than $4 million. Merrill Lynch wanted it all.

At that point Dick made a concentrated effort to pay it off. "I started pulling together funds by securing second mortgages on our Sandusky home and our condo in Florida and selling other equities, but I never sold any Cedar Fair units," Dick said.

Merrill Lynch traded the units at an historical low price. Dick said he had transferred another million dollars to them two hours before the sale, but he said they never recognized the payment and proceeded to sell the units.

The Kinzels filed a law suit against Merrill Lynch and the brokerage company's new owner, Bank of America in October 2010 and among the allegations, it claims the sale "disregarded explicit instructions" the Kinzels gave not to sell the units. The suit points out that Merrill Lynch knew the Kinzels could cover the remaining debt. Merrill Lynch was also aware, according to the suit, of the fact that "Richard and Judith Kinzel had a multiple seven-figure income which was fully protected in the event Richard Kinzel left the company voluntarily or involuntarily, by a contract which provided for payment in excess of $15 million at the time of his departure." The suit noted that the "Defendants were fully aware that the Kinzels had a top rated credit score and that they were ranked by the Merrill Lynch system as A+ credit risks."

Cedar Fair was quick to distance itself from Kinzel's troubles. "This is a personal, family matter and in no way has any bearing on, or relationship to, Cedar Fair," read the statement from Cedar Fair spokesperson Stacy Frole. "As a result, the company will not have any further comment on this matter going forward." The day that press release came out was the day Dick felt that his reputation was destroyed.

He said the news of this situation was made public and while he thinks the media reported it fairly, he was embarrassed for himself and for his entire family who read about it daily in the local newspapers. Dick finally had his days in court with the closing arguments heard in December 2014 in the Toledo Federal District Court. "It all comes down to whether the courts believe Merrill Lynch treated us in a fair and reasonable manner," Dick said. (He had not heard of any resolution as of this printing.)

The Perfect Storm of Bad Mojo

The economic downturn of 2008 had a small negative effect on park operations for Cedar Fair, but by the 2009 season, most parks around the world, including the Cedar Fair properties, were experiencing attendance and revenue downturns to varying degrees. While parks have been amazingly recession resilient over the years, most would not be so lucky this time.

Dick on the Cedar Point midway.
(Jason Werling Photo)

In 2009, attendance at the eleven amusement parks and seven water parks was down a total of 1.6 million visitors and revenues dropped nearly $80 million from 2008. The decrease in attendance was the result of a sharp decline in group sales business which was negatively affected by the poor U.S. economy, a decrease in season pass sales and poor weather in most of the markets. The revenue decline, caused by the attendance decline also represented a 1 percent decrease in per capita spending.

Plus, the company was still paying down the billion dollar-plus debt from the Paramount Parks acquisition. Upon the announcement of the poor performance, unit prices dropped to about $7, down from the $11 it had been trading at for most of the year. Along with a drop in sales, the company's shares had declined 31 percent in the previous twelve months.

As a result of the poor financial performance, Cedar Fair announced in November 2009 that it was doing away with the distribution (dividend) it had paid out to unitholders since 1987. Distributions had been reduced to one dollar per unit (share) the year before but was dropped completely in November. That ended twenty-two years of distribution in which more than a billion dollars had been distributed to Cedar Fair investors.

Earlier in the year, the company had hung "For Sale" signs on Worlds of Fun/Oceans of Fun in Kansas City and on Valleyfair in Minnesota in order to raise money to help pay down its debt but there were no takers. However, it was successful in selling off the eighty-seven acres of land next to its Canada's Wonderland park near Toronto, Ontario, Canada.

The debt load was stifling. "These problems can be traced back to a decision we made when we acquired Paramount Parks. I should have recommended a secondary offering to cover that large of a debt," Dick said. "We talked about it but the unit price was low already, so we decided to wait until the price went to a point where we could get more value out of it."

He added that the company would have been in much better shape during 2008 and 2009 had it not been for that huge debt. Dick feels most, if not all the woes the company began facing in 2009 could have been avoided if that secondary offering would have taken place. But it didn't and by the end of 2009, the company was struggling, making it a target for a buyout or takeover.

In mid-December, less than six weeks after discontinuing the dividend, the big announcement came. Cedar Fair L.P. had agreed to be acquired for $635 million by Apollo Global Management. That came out to be $11.50 a share, a 27 percent premium over the previous day's $9.08 per unit price.

Apollo's offer was unanimously approved by the board and was contingent upon two-thirds of the company's unitholder's approval and regulatory clearance. Dick felt he had a fiduciary responsibility to the unitholders to give them this opportunity to sell. The question was should Cedar Fair sell at this low price, or should it continue on its own and take a chance that it, like Six Flags, might have to declare bankruptcy and potentially leave the unitholders with nothing.

The outcry from investors was loud and public. Dick was accused of selling out at a low price, just to get the company out of debt. "If I had not put this issue in front of our investors and we would have gone bankrupt, they would have asked, even louder, why we didn't sell at $11.50 when we had the opportunity. We certainly would have ended up with a class action suit from the unitholders." Jeffrey Thomison, an equity analyst with Hilliard Lyons was quoted in various media outlets saying that the acquisition probably deserved serious consideration. "Dick Kinzel has based his career on being sensitive to shareholders. I don't think he would have done anything he felt he didn't have to do," Thomison was quoted.

Immediately following the acquisition news, Cedar Fair shares jumped 28 percent to $11.65 in aftermarket trading.

Whoa....Not so Fast!

While all this was taking place, a large Cedar Fair shareholder, Q Investments proclaimed that the company was worth much more than that and went on an aggressive campaign to sway unitholders to vote no on the sale. Dick and his team were expecting Apollo to put in a higher bid and make a play, but Apollo communicated that their bid was firm. It came down to the unitholder's decision.

Q sent out a letter on Feb. 18, 2010 telling shareholders that this was "the exact wrong time to sell the company." It went on to claim that since the transaction was announced "the bank funding markets have continued to improve." It closed on a high note saying "we are a firm believer in this company and feel that as the economy improves, it has every chance of returning to the same unit valuations it achieved before the recession."

Dick notes that the Q response to the Apollo deal actually helped Cedar Fair. "During this campaigning against our Apollo merger, Q published all our numbers and it showed we were a very good company with a good balance sheet, but with a lot of debt. That caught the attention of Wall Street and it drove our unit prices higher. Q claimed from the beginning that our company was worth more and as it turns out, they were right."

Investors were still upset with the board following its earlier decision to eliminate the cash distribution, so they were more vocal than perhaps they would have otherwise been during the Q offensive against the board. "Many of our unitholders are locals who have been investors for a long time and they love us being in Sandusky and they would have been concerned about any acquisition at any price," Dick reasoned.

After postponing the unit owner meeting at Sandusky's State Theater in which a vote was to be taken, Cedar Fair continued to push for a yes vote. Q was still campaigning for a no vote. On April 6, 2010, a few days before the re-scheduled meeting was to take place, it was announced that the deal with Apollo was terminated. In a PR Newswire release that morning, Dick explained why the deal was called off. "The board has heard from Cedar Fair unit holders and it is apparent that the merger transaction does not have the required level of investor support." It was a mutual agreement and the company was required to reimburse Apollo $6.5 million in expenses. The process also cost Cedar Fair $5.5 million in expenses.

Five years later, in a TheStreet.com story on July 21, 2015, Frederick Steier wrote of the success that Cedar Fair has had coming back from that financial crisis. He calls it a "stunning recovery" and mentions the Apollo deal that didn't happen. "Shareholders shocked the market by turning it down, and it was the best move they could have made, and possibly the best shareholder buyout rejection of all time." Steier pointed out that the units were trading at about $56 at the time of his story in mid-2015.

"Q made us look like the bad guys when all along we were just doing the right thing by communicating an opportunity. I look back now and wonder what would have happened if I hadn't taken the Apollo offer to the board, or if we had said no right from the beginning and not given our unitholders an opportunity to voice their desires. The way it played out, we gave them a choice and they turned it down."

That put Cedar Fair right back to where it was financially before the Apollo offer. In trouble. In debt. However, as the Cedar Fair board explored new options, the market became more favorable and there was now money to borrow. On May 20, 2010, the company presented its plan to refinance its $1.7 billion debt. A combination of the issuance of $500 million in unsecured bonds, taking out a $1.05 billion term loan and a $300 million line of credit would remove the uncertainty of the park's future, experts said. On hearing the news, Moody's raised Cedar Fair's rating from negative to "stable." Standard & Poor's rating also moved up to "stable."

Dick, along with two other incumbents were re-elected to continue serving on the board and the next day, the board decided to temporarily increase itself from seven to nine members to allow Q to bring in "outsiders" who they termed "new blood."

Neither the Cedar Fair board nor Dick had heard the last from Q. In early November 2010, Q went after them both personally. Q filed a request with the SEC to call a special meeting of Cedar Fair unitholders. At that meeting, Q wanted to break up the board, force Dick to resign as chairman and to force the company to increase its dividend.

To build its case to get Dick to resign, Q pointed out that it was "foolish," because of his personal investment problems, for the board to allow Dick to remain as chairman and CEO. The main focus of Q at this time was that of governance. It was their belief that the positions of chairman, president and CEO should not be under the control of one person. Q also claimed that the board was negligent for voting to allow the Apollo deal to be approved in the first place.

To apply pressure, especially on Dick, Q purchased full page advertisements in several large Northern Ohio newspapers. It was those newspaper ads that killed a big piece of Dick's spirit. "Q claimed I should be removed because I couldn't even handle my own personal investment. It was very embarrassing to me and my entire family. I worked hard all my life and gave my all to the company and then I got all this thrown at me. I felt my reputation go down the drain. It was bad. I was embarrassed."

Q put pressure on the other members of the board by threatening lawsuits against them. Q forced several members off the board who were replaced by its own candidates. Dick resigned as chairman but continued to be

Cedar Fair CEO and president until his retirement, which had already been announced. After his retirement, Dick remained on the board but due to the mandatory retirement age of board members at seventy-two, he stepped off in 2013.

He said his faith, his family and especially Judy helped him through this period. "It was very stressful and it took a lot of fire out of me. It beat me up."

The Loss of a Good Friend

As the TV pitchman always adds, "Wait, there's more."

In 1975, Dick had hired then-seasonal employee Jack Falfas as manager of park admissions and through the years, Falfas, who often called Dick his mentor, rose through the ranks. In 2005, he was brought back to Ohio from his job as VP and general manager of West Coast operations to assume the new position as COO of Cedar Fair. The new executive position was created to allow him to come back as Dick's eventual replacement. It was no secret that Dick wanted Falfas as his successor and he had communicated that desire to the board on several occasions.

That warm, decades-long friendship came to a crashing halt on June 12, 2010 during a phone conversation between Falfas and Dick. Discussion began about an MTV live show that was to travel to all the Cedar Fair parks. Dick did not like the show concept or the budget but Falfas did. What was said during that ninety-second conversation is debatable. Dick says Falfas told him he was resigning immediately. Falfas remembers Dick firing him. The company announced that Falfas had resigned but he challenged that statement and went to court seeking his job back with back pay and benefits. In April 2013 the Court of Appeals ruled that he should be reinstated.

Following several additional rulings and appeals, the case ended up in the Ohio Supreme Court and a unanimous ruling came down on Sept. 18, 2014 that while Cedar Fair owes Falfas money, the company cannot be forced to hire him back. A confidential settlement was reached between Falfas and Cedar Fair. "I don't even know what it was," Dick said, who by this time had retired and was not privy to the settlement.

It was a sad time for everyone, Dick said. "We had been friends since 1975 and I had just recommended to the board again, two days earlier that Jack replace me upon my retirement as CEO and president. Then I had to call the board and tell them Jack had just quit." Dick said Falfas was a great operations guy and was dedicated and loyal to the company and to those he worked with. "It's too bad that this bad ending had to be so public." Blogs, newspapers and fan magazines all reported on the spat between the two Cedar Fair officials. Both Dick and Falfas had huge fan bases who supported them.

"I regret the way this ended," Dick said. "I should have sat down with him and worked out a financial arrangement that was fair to him and to Cedar Fair."

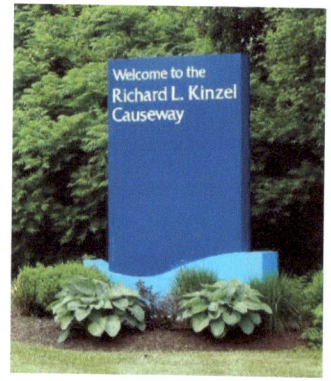

Falfas is not permitted to talk about the ordeal or the settlement directly but said there obviously was a short phone conversation and the discussion about the MTV touring show "was the straw that broke the camel's back." After spending thirty-four years with the company, the last five as the number two man behind Dick, Falfas says, "Cedar Fair is still a great part of my life and for most part, it was a great life. But it is now in my past." He is currently partners in an amusement park consulting and management company and is working on several major projects.

And He Lived Happily Ever-After

By mid-2011, the board realized that Dick's final year had been a tough one and arranged an elegant gala celebration in honor of his nearly four decades of service. "They gave me a great send-off. They knew I was pretty beat up and that my spirit had taken a strong hit, so they tried to make it up to me with this party. It was magnificent and I appreciate what everyone did for me. That was certainly the bright spot of my last few years."

Dick and Judy still live in the house they built in 1986 and they don't plan on moving, but it would be easier if they did, he thinks. The causeway from the mainland to the park was renamed the Richard L. Kinzel Causeway and crossing here is the quickest and easiest way to get to their home from Sandusky. However, Dick says at times the sight of the Cedar Point skyline, consisting of the coasters and large thrill rides he brought to the park, can be gut-wrenching. He misses his job and says that retiring changed him. Going from 100 mph to 0 mph can be tough.

Even on vacation with his family, he was always thinking about his parks. Judy laughs when she recalls that he was always in the research mode. Specifically, he had this thing about finding the perfect trash can. "We would all be having a good time and Dick would be over somewhere taking pictures of trash cans. Today, we have a great pile of trash can photos," she adds.

This reporter once asked Dick if he ever went home to have lunch with Judy since he lived only a short walk from the park. "In all those years, I never went home for lunch. Judy always told me that she married me for better or worse, but not for lunch."

With no new meaning in life, Dick says it was very depressing for the first two years after retirement. "I didn't do anything and it was really tough. Every day for nearly forty years I would get up in the morning and go to work as the sole provider and would take care of my family. My job defined who I was. I was there with advice and with financial help to my entire family when needed. Now, all of a sudden, I see Judy doing her chores and I'm sitting here watching TV," Dick said in mid-2015. "I kill time by driving around looking at things and washing the cars."

The retired lifestyle for the man who spent at least six days a week in the parks, even going to Sunday Mass during the summer in the park, has been a difficult transition. While it's getting easier, "I don't think I will ever get over all the mixed emotions I feel when I think about my career." He told a reporter in 2010 that "if God hadn't created amusement parks and given me the ability to have a vision and succeed, I'd probably be a street person."

What adds to the sadness, he says was the need to retire when he was still healthy and still loved the job and felt he could continue. "I was a healthy seventy-one, but my contract was over and the succession plan had been in place. I didn't even think about asking for another extension."

In 2007 when the board gave him a five year contract extension through the 2011 season to lead the charge to assimilate the Paramount Parks into the Cedar Fair family, Dick promised the board three things: he would work just as hard as he had the previous thirty-five years; he would have a successor ready to take over; and that he would not lobby to extend the contact beyond 2012 so they would know that he was really leaving. Dick had to adjust the succession plan when Falfas left the company, but Matt Ouimet was hired in 2011 as the heir apparent and was ready to take over for Dick in January 2012. And true to his word, Dick retired.

Being an intelligent man and knowing for at least the last five years of his contract when he would retire, one would think he would have a retirement plan. He nods his head in agreement. "I always wanted to play golf but never had the time. So when I retired, we bought a condo in Florida and I was looking forward to improving my golf game. I thought I could improve but I kept practicing and never got better. I couldn't hit the dang ball. I figured I could never learn to play well."

But he still played with his friends and "kept losing my allowance" and had realized he would never be a good player. Then one day on a particularly bad swing, his back went out and he had to give up golf. They kept the Florida condo, and they now travel back and forth several times a year, depending on the school, sports and activity schedules of their nine grandchildren. "We try to support the kids any way we can and I love attending their school events," Dick said. "It's fun for both Judy and me."

He puts his grandkids on the calendar, just as he did his own children during his busy years at the park. "I would often leave the park, pick up one or more of the kids and go to their sporting event or dance recital or whatever. I would enjoy the early evening with the family, and once they were back home, I would go back to work and finish up. I look back now with a smile and am very glad I made that decision to stay involved as they were growing up. I missed very few of their activities." On the other hand, he gives full credit to Judy for raising the kids. Did he feel guilty about not spending more time at home? "No, I never felt guilty because it has given us all the wonderful life we now have."

Best Playground in the World

All four of their children worked at the park while growing up and of course enjoyed the opportunity to play in the park as they wanted. Up until a few years ago, the nine grandchildren had the same benefits and Dick was able to impress them with his powerful position. "All these years, I've been the greatest grandpa in the world," he laughs. "In 2004 when we opened Castaway Bay the indoor waterpark, I became the greatest grandpa in the world, year-round."

Judy was always the designated tour guide when their house guests wanted to go into the park. Cedar Point was never a social thing for Dick, it was work. If he were walking with friends or family through the park and saw an issue, he would have felt compelled to leave them and address the situation then and there. "That would not have been fair to my family or friends. I was just too close. I was never able to enjoy any of our parks as a consumer."

He laughs when he adds that he may be the only dad in Northern Ohio who never took his kids to Cedar Point. They went on their own, with their friends or with their mother.

Their son Derrek, a successful executive with the Great Wolf Lodge group says the best business advice he has ever received from his father has been through action, not words. In an interview with the *Sandusky Register* in 2005, Derrek said "the best advice he's ever given me I've received through paying attention to him." He added that he and his three siblings learned three strong values from their parents: strong work ethics, love of church, and love for family and country.

Following his retirement, Dick was asked to consult on various park projects. He is not interested. He has been asked to run for political office. He's not interested. People knowing of his success have asked for donations. He and Judy have been particular, but generous with their personal philanthropy.

He also believed in strong corporate philanthropy. During his years with Cedar Fair, Dick made sure the company did what it could to help out in the community and those efforts speak loudly. His ties with Sandusky, where he chose to keep Cedar Fair headquarters, went beyond just living and working in the community. United Way, Salvation Army, the American Red Cross and Give Kids the World are just a few causes on the long list of philanthropy and fund-raising projects Cedar Point and he and Judy personally have helped.

In December 2014, he and Judy committed $1 million to the Sandusky Central Catholic School, the largest gift ever given to that school. The money went toward the update of school buildings and public spaces and major updates to the gymnasium, which has been renamed the Kinzel Center. Dick points out that this was a gift of money AND of his guidance. "I just didn't want to hand them a check and let them decide how to use it. I believe in charity, but I don't believe that 10 percent or more should go to administration." The million dollar gift came with a stipulation. Dick was to see all bills and oversee how and what gets paid from he and Judy's donation. The school readily accepted the guidelines.

Father Michael Roemmele of Sandusky Central Catholic High School shows Dick and Judy around the new Kinzel Center at the school.
(Luke Wark Photo)

Similar guidelines were placed on the couple's "several thousand dollar" 2015 donation to the Boys & Girls Club of Erie County. It will be used to build a multi-purpose sports court for the Teen Center located in Sandusky. "We want to do more charity work in the future. It is always nice to be able to give back to our community, especially when you have been as fortunate as Judy and I."

Judy makes a point that Dick's success is not all about power and money, it's also about his strong personal values. "Dick has always stayed true to his values. He values his relationship with God and never misses Mass. He values his family and even when he was the busiest, very seldom missed an event in our children's life. He valued everyone he worked with, kept an open-door policy and he truly understood everyone's value to Cedar Fair. He valued his health by jogging five miles every morning, and he always valued honesty and never made a promise he couldn't keep."

One person Dick particularly valued was Brenda Lakner, his administrative assistant for all his years as CEO. She was Bob Munger's administrative assistant and Dick inherited her when he got the job. "She scheduled her entire personal life around my business schedule. It was not always easy. Whenever I needed her, she was there and ready to help."

Over the years, both Dick and Cedar Point received a great deal of press from the local daily newspaper, the *Sandusky Register*. While the reporters were honest and didn't play favorites, they were kind hearted and fair to the hometown's leading employer. In a 2003 story entitled "Kinzel's the Point Man," the paper summed up Dick's career. "Dick Kinzel was just a boy from Toledo. No college degree. No ties to Sandusky. He had never even visited Cedar Point ... His first day he made cotton candy. Now, he makes $1 million a year. Dick Kinzel was just a boy from Toledo. Now, he's a legend – in Sandusky and around the country."

Dick smiled when he read that and noted that "Yes, I am known in Sandusky, but that sometimes gets awkward, like when I am out to eat or at a grocery store and someone comes up and asks me to get their kid a job." Most of the time, he adds. "It's really nice. This is our home." The locals always respected Dick and Judy's private, personal lives. "In all of our years in Sandusky, even with our telephone number being printed in the book, I only received one call where an individual called my home to register a complaint."

Dick's peers have always been quick to recognize his accomplishments. The most meaningful of his kudos and accolades over the years was his 2006 induction into the IAAPA Hall of Fame. Out of all the letters of support for his Hall of Fame nomination, the praise from Joe Heflin, VP of sales for Whitewater West Industries, showed the most love and admiration. "His parks are spotless, beautifully landscaped, staffed with enthusiastic and proud employees who care about what you think. Each park truly is his own. He has brought his love and life to our industry contributing more than anyone else to the positive image we now receive from the public."

Heflin closes out with a direct request to put Dick into the Hall of Fame. "I believe we owe it to him to show our appreciation for what he has done for us. No one has had more love, more passion and more impact on our industry than Dick Kinzel." Dozens of similar letters of praise were received from industry leaders from around the world.

Dick and Don Miears accepted the prestigious Applause Award for Cedar Point in 1996 during the IAAPA Convention and Trade Show in Orlando. (Tim O'Brien Photo)

Jack Falfas, then COO of Cedar Fair, wrote that Dick was "a man of his word, a man of honor, and he has served as an excellent role model for many of us at Cedar Fair and in the industry as well. Dick is a friend and a mentor, but he is also a dean of this industry."

Two years after being inducted into the IAAPA Hall of Fame, the group honored him again, with the Lifetime Service Award which recognizes an individual's consistent and long-term achievements.

Another major industry award came just months before his retirement. In its September 2011 issue, *Amusement Today* honored Dick with its first-ever Living Legend award, praising not only his vision in building the biggest and best roller coasters over the years, but for his restive spirit in insisting on only the best of everything for his ever-expanding collection of parks. In that same issue, *Amusement Today* announced that Cedar Point had, for the fourteenth consecutive year, won the Golden Ticket Award for Best Park in the world, as voted by fans worldwide. While not specifically an award for Dick, the Best Park kudo would not have been possible without his thirty-nine years of vision and foresight.

Dick and his granddaughter Maddie celebrated his honorary degree from Bowling Green State University.

Under his management and leadership, Cedar Point won the prestigious international Applause Award in 1996, a general excellence award presented every two years by a Board of Governors of industry experts. Cedar Point was in competition with every park in the world for that award.

In Donald Trump's 2004 book, *The Way to the Top – The Best Business Advice I Ever Received,* Dick is featured as one of the 150 top businesspeople who offer "a range of inspiring and practical advice on making good decisions" as a leader. Dick writes about greed, both in business and in one's personal life. "Pigs get fat and hogs get slaughtered. Businesses, empires and families can be destroyed by greed. In business, greed can manifest itself in pricing, investing and capital expenditures. In one's personal life, greed can cause a lack of balance between professional responsibilities and family obligations. Ultimately, greed can be controlled by using good common sense."

Ernst & Young named him Entrepreneur of the Year for Northwest Ohio and shortly after that in 1998, he received an honorary doctorate degree from Bowling Green State University for his outstanding business achievements. The program introduced him thusly: "Richard Kinzel is in the production business. He makes fun. He mass produces laughter and screams of joy. He is a smile-maker by trade."

Dick is quick to admit that the smiles on his face and the fun in his heart were scarce the last few years. The lawsuits and retirement have been miserable for him, but he says he can't complain about his life nor is he compelled to say anything bad about the company he loved and worked for all these years. "We've been blessed and we have all had a great life. Working for this company has provided a beautiful lifestyle for my entire family."

About that coaster war he started?

He won it.

Big time.

SELECTED BIBLIOGRAPHY

"Amusement Today Honors Richard Kinzel as Living Legend," *Amusement Today*, September 2011

Barhite, Brandi, "Cedar Fair Top Exec in Line for Last Ride," *Sandusky Register*

Brown, LaRaye, "Dragster May Mean Tourism Record," *Sandusky Register*, Feb. 11, 2003

Cartmell, Robert, *The Incredible Scream Machine, A History of the Roller Coaster*, Amusement Park Books/Bowling Green State University Press, 1987

"Cedar Fair and Affiliates of Apollo Global Management Mutually Terminate Merger Agreement," PR Newswire-First Call, April 6, 2010

Cedar Fair Annual Reports, 1986-2012

Cedar Fair Press Releases, 1985-2015

"Cedar Fair, L.P. (FUN)," *CEO Interviews*, Aug. 6, 1990

"Cedar Fair's CEO Dick Kinzel Shares Thoughts on Paramount Deal," *Amusement Today*, July 2006

Chavez, Jon, "Financial Roller Coaster," *The Blade*, Nov. 11, 2007

Chavez, Jon, "Is Bigger Really Better at Point?" *The Blade*, Aug. 1, 1999

Falfas, Jack, interview with Tim O'Brien by telephone, July 25, 2015

Francis, David W. and Diane, *Cedar Point, The Queen of American Watering Places*, revised edition, 2009

Goldberg, Steven T., "What Goes Up..." *Kiplinger's Personal Finance Magazine*, August 1996

Gubernick, Lisa, "Terror with a Smile," *Forbes*, Sept. 3, 1991

Guide to Ride, a Guide to the Roller Coasters of North America, American Coasters Enthusiasts, 2000

Hildebrandt, John, Interview with Tim O'Brien, in Sandusky, Ohio, June 4, 2015

Hirsch, Jerry, "Knott's Berry Farm Sold," *The Orange County Register*, Oct. 22, 1997

"IAAPA 2000: Dick Kinzel Interview," Parts one and two, Coasterbuzz.com, Nov. 15 & 16, 2000

Jackson, Tom, "Like Father, Like Son," *Sandusky Register*, Feb. 20, 2005

Jackson, Tom, "Cedar Fair CEO Sues Merrill Lynch, Bank of America," *Sandusky Register*, Oct. 16, 2010

Jewett, Lee, Interview with Tim O'Brien, in Sandusky, Ohio, June 4, 2015

Johnston, Christopher, "Business is a Pleasure on the Midway," *Cleveland Enterprise*, summer 1994

Kinzel, Richard, Interviews with Tim O'Brien, in Sandusky, Ohio, June 3 & 4, 2015; and numerous discussions by telephone, June 15 – Sept. 30, 2015

Lococo, Gasper, Interview with Tim O'Brien, by telephone, July 13, 2015

Miears, Don, Interview with Tim O'Brien, by telephone, Aug. 19, 2015

"Maverick by Name, Maverick by Nature," Editorial, *Sandusky Register*, Sept. 14, 2006

Moschke, Will, "Cedar Point Lighthouse Beckons for 150 Years," *Roller Coaster*, summer 2012

Munarriz, Rick Aristotle, "Cedar Fair Restamps Kinzel's Hand," *The Motley Fool*, Dec. 22, 2006

O'Brien, Tim, *Legends: Pioneers of the Amusement Park Industry*, Ripley Entertainment, 2007

O'Brien, Tim, "New Cedar Point Ride Cloaked in Mystery," *Amusement Business*, Oct. 14, 2002

O'Brien, Tim, "Cedar Point Officials $25 Million Ride a Home Run," *Amusement Business*, May 19, 2003

O'Brien, Tim, "Resort Side to Take Center Stage in Cedar Point's Expansion Plans," *Amusement Business*, Nov. 17, 2003

O'Brien, Tim, "Managing from the Heart," *Funworld*, April 2005

O'Brien, Tim, "Kinzel: Cedar Fair Parks Intend to Stay Biggest, Best," *Amusement Business*, Sept. 16, 1996

O'Brien, Tim, "Cedar Fair CEO Discusses Challenges Ahead," *Amusement Business*, July 1, 2002

"Q Funding Sends Letter to Cedar Fair Unitholders Urging Them to Vote Against the Pending Transaction with Apollo Global Management," Business Wire, Feb. 18, 2011

Ruben, Paul, "Cedar Point's Record Breaker," *Parkworld*, September 2000

Samavati, Shaheen, "Cedar Fair Outlines Plans to Refinance its $1.7 Billion Debt," *The Plain Dealer*, May 21, 2010

Schoolfield, Jeremy, "Changing the Landscape," *Funworld,* June, July, August, 2007

Shick, Alan, Interview with Tim O'Brien, on the Cedar Point midway, June 5, 2015

Taulli, Tom, "Apollo and Cedar Fair Abandon a $2.4 Billion Leveraged Buyout," Daily Finance.com, April 7, 2010

Throgmorton, Todd H., *Roller Coasters of America,* Motorbooks International Publishers, 1994

Throne, Michael, "The Point's Lost on Banshee," *Sandusky Register,* Sept. 18, 1995

Trump, Donald, *The Way to the Top,* Crown Business, 2004

Wyatt, Mark, *White Knuckle Ride,* Salamander Books, 1996

ACKNOWLEDGEMENTS

First of all, a huge thank you goes out to Dick and Judy Kinzel. They welcomed me as Dick's official biographer and they graciously opened their home and their archives to me as I began this journey to capture the life and times of the Roller Coaster King of Cedar Point Amusement Park. Their cooperation was not only welcomed, but it was essential in this process.

There is no shortage of written material about Dick's thirty-nine years with Cedar Point and Cedar Fair and I tried to read and research as much of it as possible. I was impressed with the depth of coverage Cedar Point's local newspaper, the *Sandusky Register* gave Dick, Cedar Point and Cedar Fair over the years. The publication's past writings were well written and quite valuable in my research.

Cedar Fair's Lee Alexakos found some great photos in the Cedar Point archives that I have used in the book and Jason Werling of the *Sandusky Register* provided several photos to this project as well. I credited the photographer when possible, but unfortunately many of the photos I found in Dick's archives did not have the photographer's name attached and I am unable to give credit.

Thank you also goes out to Lee Jewett, John Hildebrandt, Gasper Lococo, Paul Ruben, Tim Baldwin, and Alan Shick for their time and insights along the way.

And of course, I acknowledge you, the reader and the buyer of this book. Thanks for doing your part to help us capture and preserve the stories of the *Legends & Legacies* of the amusement park industry!

ABOUT THE AUTHOR

Tim O'Brien has been chronicling the amusement park and outdoor entertainment industry for more than four decades. During that time, the award-winning photojournalist has had more than 5,000 articles, 3,000 photos, and 16 books published.

In addition to *Dick Kinzel - Roller Coaster King of Cedar Point Amusement Park*, Tim's books include: *Tony Baxter - First of the Second Generation of Walt Disney Imagineers*; *The Amusement Park Guide*; *The Wave Maker - Story of Theme Park Pioneer George Millay*; *Legends - Pioneers of the Amusement Park Industry*; *Ward Hall - King of the Sideshow*; and *Ripley's Believe It or Not! Amusement Park Oddities & Trivia*.

Tim and his wife Kathleen live in Nashville, Tenn. with their two cats, George Harrison and Petula Clark.

ABOUT THE *LEGENDS & LEGACIES* SERIES

A timeless wisdom energizes the world's greatest entertainment venues – theme parks, amusement parks, fairs, carnivals, circuses, sideshows, museums and unique one-of-a-kind attractions.

The *Legends & Legacies* series is a quick and easy read about the innovators and their insights and secrets who created these irresistible pleasure palaces. Expertly written by award winning photojournalist Tim O'Brien, the biographies and histories reveal the best of those who spent a lifetime delivering smiles, fun and laughter, all while creating value.

Each person chronicled in this series has been personally interviewed extensively by the author and the story is based on that primary research, with some help from secondary research that was vetted for its accuracy.

Each volume is filled with valuable insights and lessons in creative leadership from the greatest builders and dreamers of all time.

ACE, 30, 31
Alexakos, Lee, 61, 119
Apollo Global, 100 - 104, 116, 118
Applause Award, 113, 114
Arrow Development, 6, 14, 16
Avalanche Run, 30, 37

B&M, 40, 41, 54, 55, 92
Banshee, 42 - 44, 118
Beast, 38, 92
Behemoth, 92
Berenstain Bear Country, 37
Bolliger, Walter, 40, 41, 54
Bonfante Gardens, 90
Breakers Express, 61
Breakers Tower, 61

California's Great America, 90
Camp Snoopy, 45, 77
Canada's Wonderland, 90, 92, 94, 100
Canteen, 7, 8, 21
Carolina Cobra, 92
Carowinds, 55, 90, 92, 93, 94
Castaway Bay, 61, 63, 109
Cedar Fair, 5 -115
Cedar Point, 5 - 115
Challenge Park, 60
Coaster Mania, 55, 56
Corkscrew, 6, 13 - 15, 20

Derrough, Lee 74
Dinn, Charles, 38
Disaster Transport, 37, 38
Dominator, 92
Dorney Park, 37, 44, 70 - 77, 96

Falfas, Jack, 33, 34, 78, 88, 105, 106, 108, 114, 116
Firehawk, 92
Fury 325, 55, 93

Gatekeeper, 29, 55

Geauga Lake, 48, 67, 82, 85 - 87, 92
Gemini, 16, 30
GhostRider, 78
Gilroy Gardens, 90
Golden Ticket Awards, 56, 114
Great Coasters International, 53
Great Wolf Lodge, 61, 90, 110

Hanna-Barbera, 93, 94
Headspin, 92
Heflin, Joe, 113
Hercules, 72, 73
Hildebrandt, John, 34, 36, 42, 60, 61, 62, 77, 117, 119
Hotel Breakers, 44, 58, 61, 63, 65
Hunt, Lamar, 74
Huss Park Attractions, 51

IAAPA, 26, 49, 84, 112, 113, 117
Intamin, 30, 46, 48, 50, 52, 54, 92
Intimidator, 92
Intimidator 305, 92
Iron Dragon, 30, 31

Jasper, Monty, 46, 47, 54
Jewett, Lee, 13 - 15, 26, 28, 29, 31, 36, 119
Jourdan, Roger, 82

Kalahari Resort, 61
Keller, Dan, 73, 74
Kernacs, Sandor, 46, 54
Key Bank, 23
Kings Dominion, 90, 92, 93, 94
Kings Island, 17, 38, 44, 51, 88, 90 - 94
Kinzel Center at Sandusky Central Catholic High School, 111
Kinzel, Judy, 4, 7, 11, 18, 19, 28, 29, 53, 74, 84, 97, 104, 107, 109, 110, 111, 119

121

Knott's Berry Farm, 14, 69, 70, 75, 78, 80, 90, 117
Knott's Camp Snoppy, 77
Knott's Soak City, U.S.A., 79, 80

Lazard Financial, 23, 24
Legros., Emile, 12, 58, 59
Lighthouse Point, 61, 62
Lococo, Gasper, 67, 68, 87, 117, 119

Magnum XL-200, 5, 30, 31 - 35, 44
Mamba, 44, 74
Mantis, 41, 43, 44
Marriott Parks, 11
Masterson, Bob, 26
Maverick, 51 - 53, 117
MaXair, 51
Mean Streak, 38, 39, 53, 54, 72
Merrill Lynch, 97, 98, 117
Michigan's Adventure, 76, 82
Miears, Don, 40, 73, 117
Millennium Force, 45 - 47
Mondial Rides, 54
Morey, Jack, 54
Morgan Mfg, 44
Munger, Bob, 12 - 19, 23, 24, 27, 30, 37, 58, 59, 69, 86, 112

Near, Bill, 8, 11, 72, 73
New York Stock Exchange, 24
Nickelodeon, 77, 93, 94

Oasis Water Park, 79
Opryland, 14
Ouimet, Matt, 108

Paramount Parks, 88, 90 - 100, 108, 116
Peanuts, 37, 45, 77, 82
Premier Parks, 85, 87
Prowler, 53

Q Investments, 101 - 104, 118

Radisson Harbour Hotel, 63
Raptor, 40, 41
Renegade, 53
Richard L. Kinzel Causeway, 58, 107
Roose, George, 12, 58, 59, 60, 69
Rougarou, 42

Sandcastle Suites, 36, 61
Shivering Timbers, 82
Six Flags, 31, 40, 57, 72, 81 - 88, 101
Skyhawk, 51
Soak City, 36, 60
Speigel, Dennis, 91
Star Trek: The Experience, 90
Steel Force, 44
Steel Venom, 48

Thunderhawk, 82
Toomer, Ron, 14 - 16, 31, 32, 54
Top Thrill Dragster, 48 - 51, 62
Trump, Donald, 115
Twister, 48

Valleyfair, 7, 17, 18 - 23, 30, 36, 37, 44, 53, 65, 67, 69, 73, 81, 100
Veit, David, 23, 35
Vekoma, 45, 82, 92
Visionland, 80

Wabash Cannonball, 13, 15
Walt Disney World, 8, 22
Wasserman, Lou, 17
Weinstein, Harris, 72, 73
Wild Thing, 44
Wildwater Kingdom, 86
Wolverine Wildcat, 82
Woodworth, Truman, 12
Worlds of Fun, 44, 53, 70, 73, 74, 76, 100

www.ingramcontent.com/pod-product-compliance
Lightning Source LLC
Chambersburg PA
CBHW042057290426
44112CB00001B/6